Sector Rotation:

High Profit and Low Risk

Tony Pow

Why you want to read this book

- I have been attacked by my competitor or just a racist on this book. Even before the new edition of the book was available, I had a bad review. I am making this book very affordable until the bully ends. Return the book (check out the return policy) if it is that bad or it does not fit your purpose. Otherwise, I'll appreciate an honest review.

- My annuity has grown **four** times since I started using sector rotation. How many authors can say that? None to my knowledge.

- I have **11** strategies in sector rotation while most books have only one. It ranges from simple rotation of a stock ETF and cash to finding best stocks in best sectors.

- As of 4/2016, I had switched 80% of this account to cash based on the technical indicator. I switched most (if not all) my sector funds in April, 2000 from technology sectors to traditional sectors (better to money market fund). We can reduce losses by spotting market plunges (Chapter 2) and spotting the sector trend.

- As of 9/25/15, I glanced through my competing books in Kindle format. Here are my personal comments and check whether it makes sense to you.

  - ETF Rotation. 3.5 stars. **91** pages. $9.99.
  - Super Sectors. 3.5 stars. 264 pages. $26.39.
  - Profiting from ETF Rotation. 3.5 stars. **35** pages. $7.55. Must be reviewed by friends or it is very, very concisely great.
  - Standard & Poor's Sector Investing. 3 stars. 260 pages **$97.58**.
  - Dual Momentum Investing. 5 stars. 240 pages. $34.99. After reading several of the comments and the table of contents, I only found only one chapter is useful to me. The absolute momentum and relative momentum have been described in my book.

My book has about 265 pages (solid information and nothing on my life to fill the pages) and the Kindle version only costs $6.95 and paperback is also available. Please confirm it whether I am wrong or just I am naturally biased.

- Most books on this topic do not consider cash or money market fund as a sector. The average loss in the last two market plunges is about 45%. When the market is plunging, cash is the best investment.

- I select proven ideas from more than 100 books besides my original ideas and experiences.

- Many 100-page books could turn into just a few pages of useful information after the narrating the story of the author's life.

- My articles in SeekingAlpha.com. I claim to have the best one-year performance of any articles for recommending 5 or more stocks.
http://seekingalpha.com/article/2492255-a-tale-of-2-portfolios

My motivation to write this book is sharing my experiences, both bad and good. I provide simple-to-follow techniques using the free (or low-cost) resources available to us. I have been successful in investing for decades. I am enjoying a comfortable financial life. I do not hold back my 'secrets' as my children are not interested in investing. It is my small legacy in sharing my investing ideas.

If you are looking how to make 100% return overnight, there are many other books claiming to do so and this book is not for you. This book describes how to be a 'turtle' investor making fortune gradually and surely. Be warned that many books written by authors who have never make money in the stock market.

As everything in life, there is no guarantee that this book will make you money. However, the chance of success will be substantially improved especially when you practice on most of the ideas presented in this book.

Sector rotation in a nutshell

How to start

I have been rotating sectors in my annuity for quite a long time and this strategy has increased about four times over the years. My employer had a lot of restrictions for me to trade stocks, so switching sector funds in my annuity was the best investment for me. When your account grows to a large amount, it is better to use a subscription service to determine the rankings of sectors (Chapter 31).

For starter, I recommend to paper test your strategy. Use Finviz.com to select the best performing sector and/or use my quick analysis of ETFs (Chapter 6). Switch it every month (or two) to the ETF corresponding to the best sector. Again, switch to cash when the market is risky (Chapter 2).

After the basic, this book provides many features to further refine your strategy. Use Technical Analysis (Chapter 8-10). Start with the technical indicators such as SMA-50% and RSI(14) and a handful of sector ETFs to rotate (suggested sectors are technology, bank, health care, housing, consumer and material).

In addition, some sectors are more profitable in different phases of a market cycle. We examine several industry sectors and country sectors in more detail. The rise of China is affecting the global economy. When the interest rate is low, it would affect bonds and stocks yielding high dividends.

Many books ignore market timing. It turns out to be the most important as the last market plunges have an average loss of 45%!

The key to profitable sector rotation

Sector rotation could be very profitable and less risky than most of us expect. There are two ways to profit:

1. Buy when the sector is trending up and sell when the sector is trending down. It is the common approach to sector rotation.

2. Buy at the bottom of a sector and sell at the peak. It is hard to detect the bottom/peak. It will be briefly described next.

The following is the very basic way to rotate sectors. Many investment subscriptions and free sites such as finviz.com select favorable sectors every month. We assume the best-performed sector last month will perform better in the coming month. It does not always happen such as the tech sector in April, 2000 and the reversed direction of drug sector in 2015. To protect your investment, use mental stops to avoid flash crashes.

Alternatively, we can select them via simple charts as described in this book. Beginners should start with Single Moving Average. Using more than one technical indicator without understanding them completely could cost you money.

Detecting the bottom of a sector

It is not easy and no one can detect the bottom or the peak of a sector consistently. The SMA-350 (Single Moving Average with 350 sessions) detects the market quite accurately for the last two market plunges. I have tested out the "days" with different numbers and 350 is the best fit for the last two market plunges.

Besides technical indicators, there are hints that indicate a sector is close to the bottom. Use the ETF for the sector and check out the fundamental metrics similar to evaluating a stock. To illustrate, enter XLE in Yahoo!Finance or finviz.com to get the current price and other info about this sector.

Calculate the percentage of its current price from the bottom in the last 350 trade sessions. We assume the last bottom should be close to the next bottom in a sideway market. The intangibles should be considered too.

Detecting the trend

Detecting the trend is easier than detecting the bottom/peak. To illustrate, bring up finviz.com from your browser and enter XLE. For most sectors, I use the SMA-50 (50-day single moving average), which is readily available as one of the metrics. When the stock price is 3% above SMA, buy. When it is 3% below the SMA, sell. It is simple, but it has been proven many times.

You can adjust the 50-day and the 3% (some use 1%) to how long your average holding period of an ETF or a stock and how often you want to trade. If your holding period is longer, use higher number such as 90 days. If you want to trade more often use 1% instead of 3%.

Personally I use 60 days if I use charts (from Yahoo!Finance among one of the many free sites that provide charts). One of my accounts requires 60 days for minimum holding period without incurring a fee.

To detect market crashes and when to reenter the market or a sector ETF or a mutual fund after the crash, I use 350 days (some use 300 days). The 'days' is actually trade sessions.

RSI(14) indicates whether the sector is overbought or oversold. RSI oscillates between zero and 100. Traditionally, and according to Wilder, RSI is considered overbought with a value above 70 and oversold with a value below 30 as described in the article. This indicator is available from Finviz.com.

   (http://stockcharts.com/school/doku.php?id=chart_school:technical_indicators:relative_strength_index_rsi)

A simple way is to buy last month's winner(s). Ensure the ETFs are not leveraged if you are conservative. Include contra ETFs when the market is risky for aggressive investors.

What to buy

I prefer ETFs for specific sectors and sector funds (check out the holding period to exit without penalties) are another choice. Sector funds are better than ETFs in specific sectors such as banking, drug companies and mining.

ETFs charge less for maintaining and they have all the advantages of a stock. However, mutual funds select the stocks within a sector selectively. Fidelity offers the most complete sector mutual funds. Compare the 3 or 5 year performance between the ETF and the sector fund in this same sector.

The third option is top-down approach. First, when the market is not plunging, select the favorable sector and then the stocks within the sector. Many free sites provide a filter for favorable sectors.

Here is a list of sector ETFs.
(http://www.bloomberg.com/markets/etfs/)

Here is a list of commission-free ETFs from Fidelity.
(https://www.fidelity.com/etfs/ishares)

Some sector funds automatically switch sectors for you. My experience did not prove to me to be profitable. Check out their past performance.

Favorable sectors according to the market cycle

Refer the chapter on Market Timing and Spotting Market Plunge for specific strategies. I remind myself to close most positions when the market is plunging.

Favorable sectors according to the interest rate

It is similar to the above. Retailing, auto and housing are usually hurt by high interest rates. However, the improving economy would take out this disadvantage as more employed folks can afford big-ticket items.

Favorable sectors according to geography

It is not an easy task. China and India had their best performing years. Japan had one of the best years in 2013 during the two decades. For foreign countries, currency fluctuation should be considered. Most emerging countries have their ups and downs. Most ETFs or sector funds buy larger companies that are more trustworthy in the financial statements.

Global economies have never been that tightly connected. When the US economy is down, China is affected and so are the resource-rich countries.

Favorable and unfavorable events

The EU crisis has been taken more than three years as of 4/2016 and the EU stocks are still close to the bottom. I prefer to buy an ETF specialized in EU or a mutual fund when the trend is up.

When the Treasury says the interest will be lower, the market and the long term bond funds will move up, and vice versa. To me, the interest rate will move up slowly from the 1/2014 bottom. Most likely the new Fed chairwoman will not raise the interest rate until the economy totally recovers.

Recent favorable and unfavorable sectors

There are many sources to check what sectors perform recently. Finviz.com is one of them. From the top menu bar, select Group, and the best and worst sectors will be displayed. Skip one day or one week unless you have special interest on these short durations. Select the duration depending on your purpose. Personally I would use one month (or two) for my monthly rotation strategy betting the momentum would pass to the next month.

Technical analysis would spot the trend. Select Simple Moving Average with n-day. It is similar to the TA used in the chapter spotting market crash. Instead of using SPY or another ETF market index, use an ETF that represents the sector.

Sector rotation by fund managers

We cannot beat these institution investors. We need to follow them or one step ahead of them. They rotate sectors when they find another sector has better appreciation potential or the current favorable sector has reached its peak.

When to rotate
Rotate for the following reasons:

1. When the market is plunging, rotate the sector ETFs and/or mutual funds to cash. Aggressive investors would rotate their equities to contra ETFs. The average loss of the last two market plunges is about 45%. This chart will not determine the peak as it depends on the falling data. However, it will tell you when to exit to prevent further loss and tell you when to reenter the market.

2. When the fundamentals of the current sector bought are turning bad.

3. When there is another sector that has better appreciation potential. Finviz.com tells you the rankings of the sectors.

4. When the sector is overbought or peaking, and / or has met our objective.

Do not forget market timing

Do NOT buy any stocks except the contra ETFs when the market is plunging. Playing defense usually wins the game more often than playing offense. You can make good money without sector rotation by following market timing. When the market is peaking, protect your profits by placing stop loss orders.

Positions and how often to switch

It depends on the size of your portfolio and how much time you can afford to monitor your portfolio. To me, it varies from 2 to 6 positions and 20 to 90 days to monitor the switches.

Statistics show that a portfolio with 5 positions rotating in 20 days give you slightly better performance and less drawback (maximum loss for the period). I recommend 4 (2 for a portfolio of less than $20,000) and 30 days (and 60 days for Fidelity sector funds).

Conclusion

Sector rotation is described in very basic terms here. The links in Afterthoughts provide additional information.

As a reminder, roughly half of a stock's price movement can be attributed to the sector it is in.

Afterthoughts

- There are many articles in this topic. They are:

  Sector rotation strategies ETF investors must know. There are many useful links.
  http://www.bloomberg.com/markets/etfs/

  Sector rotation based on performance.
  http://stockcharts.com/school/doku.php?id=chart_school:tradi ng_strategies:sector_rotation_roc
  Fidelity on Sectors.
  https://www.fidelity.com/sector-investing/overview
  Video instruction.
  http://www.youtube.com/watch?v=j5yYoOoATRM

- No one can consistently predict the bottom or the peak of any sector. Sometimes we move in too early and lose another 25% or so, or we leave the sector too early to lose another 25% or so potential gain. It is quite normal. Learn it why we move in the wrong time, and a lot of times it is just bad luck or events beyond our control.

- A free (as of this writing) service on sector rotation.
  http://www.gosector.com/

Related Topics:

###

Specialize in a sector

When you work in a sector or you're interested in a specific sector, you may want to specialize in that sector for investing. High tech is a popular sector. You need to specialize in a growing sector unless you short stocks.

With aging population, health care is a good one. With growing population, commodities and agribusiness (including water) are good sectors.

Major sectors: Consumer Discretionary, Consumer Staple, Energy, Financial (banks, insurances, brokers), Heath Care (including drugs), Industrial, Material, Technology and Utilities. They are sub divided into many subsectors (a.k.a. industries).

For more information on a sector, google it. This link is an example describing all industries within the health care sector.

Outline on how to start

1. First determine your risk tolerance, how much time you have for investing, your knowledge in investing/your desire in learning investing and your portfolio size. If the above is limited, SPY or any ETF simulating the market is your only sector and market timing is your primary tool (Chapter 2). You can stop here for now.

2. Refer to Chapter 4 for sector ETFs and mutual funds to rotate.

3. There are at least 2 simple ways to select which ETF or mutual fund to rotate to: Technical Analysis / Fundamental Analysis and subscription services. You can identify the current favorable sectors from finviz.com, cnnfn.com and fidelity.com (their customers only).

4. Paper test your strategy (chosen from one or more of the above).

5. When it is thoroughly tested out and the result is good, use real money slowly and gradually. Monitor your performance.

The rest of the book describes the other aspects in sector rotation such as Top-Down Investing (in case you prefer to find the stocks in the favorable sector), country sectors, specific industry sectors... Many investing ideas described here are applicable to other investing strategies.

Strategies for sector rotations

Most books on Sector Rotation have one strategy so it is easy to follow. I recommend glancing thru the entire book. Then select the recommended strategy depending on your knowledge, your risk tolerance and available time for research.

We have 11 strategies in sector rotation from simple market timing to rotate between SPY and cash to the more complicated ones. You can combine the strategies such as Strategy #1 and #8. Many strategies share common topics such as ETF Analysis. Because of this, the flow of the book is not linear and appears to be more complicated. However, this edition tries to flow as linear as possible.

Besides market timing and finding last month's best-performed sector, some sectors reverse their trend very fast. To limit market loss, use stop orders (i.e. when the price falls into a specific value, sell it via a market order). When the market is peaking, I prefer not to own it or am more cautious. Many learned it the hard way during the internet crash in 2000 and the recent bio tech crash.

Start with one (rotate between SPY and cash recommended) and use a virtual account from one of the free sites such as Investopedia. Here are my 11 strategies.

1. Rotate 2 sectors (Section I): SPY (or any ETF that simulates the market) and cash (or a short-term bond ETF or contra ETF for aggressive investors).
   - "Power of market timing" should convince you.
   - Chapter 2-3 determines when to switch. Takes only minutes a month.

- Recommend this strategy with other strategies. When the market plunges, most sectors go down.

2. Rotate 4 ETFs (Section II).
   - Aggressive investors can add a contra ETF.
   - Add additional sector ETFs to diversify.
   - Rotate your current ETF to the one that performed best last month.

3. Rotate from more sectors using Strategy #2 but use a specific sector ETF instead of SPY. Select the best-performed sector. There are many free sites to show what one performs the best last month such as cnnfn.com and SeekingAlpha.com. To spread out the rest, select the top two sector ETFs instead of one.

4. Select sectors according to stages of a market cycle (Section IV).
5. Select country sectors that perform the best last month (Section V).
6. Sectors by asset class (Sector VI).
7. Market correction (Sector VII). Buy at temporary dips and sell at temporary peaks. When the market is plunging, sell most holdings.
8. According to the calendar.
9. According to the interest rate.
10. According to subscription service. If your investment is large such as over $100,000, subscribe an investment newsletter on sector selection costing about $100. Use the techniques described in this book as a second opinion.
11. Top-down investing (Section XI).
    The problem of ETFs is ETFs include bad stocks in the sector indiscriminately. After a better sector has been spotted, search for the good stocks within the sector. The other problem is ETFs include too many 'bubble' stocks.

Contents

Introduction

Sector rotation has been proven to make good profits at the least risk if it is properly implemented. This book improves your odds in making profits than traditional schemes in sector rotation by:

- Market Timing. When the market is plunging, do not buy any stock including sector ETFs and sector funds. This book provides a simple chart to detect market plunges (Chapter 2). Basically it is a sector rotation between SPY (an ETF that simulates the market) and cash (or an ETF of short-term bonds).

- The next rotation strategy involves four ETFs in a rising market described in Chapter 4. Optionally, you can include a contra ETF to time the market. Buy the best performer of last month of the selected ETFs.

- Some sectors perform better in different stages of a market cycle as described in Chapter 12 and 13.

- Many free sites describe the best sector performers such as Seeking Alpha and CNNfn.

- Evaluate sector using Technical Analysis (simple charts available free from the web described in Chapter 8-11) and Fundamental Analysis. Use the same tools to evaluate individual stocks within a performing sector – top-down investing.

- You should spend one hour or two a month to determine which sector to rotate to or move your portfolio to cash when the market is risky. The "Buy and hold" strategy does not perform since 2000.

- Subscription services (Chapter 31-32). There are many. Even if you subscribe these services, you should read this book to evaluate their services and use this book as a second opinion. When your portfolio is over $100,000, $100 for a yearly subscription should pay itself in the long run.

- Market timing by calendar and presidential cycle.

- My recent experiences in sector trading.

- Be careful on many books on this topic were written by professors who may never make a buck in the stock market.

- Some "best" sellers were written more than 10 years ago that do not have today's basic tools such as technical analysis and bear any resemblance to today's market, which can be manipulated by institution investors.

- Most large companies today are global companies. The importance in investing foreign companies to diversify is less important than before.

- When China expands, natural resource-rich countries would most likely benefit.

- Most similar books have one strategy and this book has 11 strategies. You can combine the strategies such as market timing with last month's best-performed sector.

Besides industrial sectors, I include bonds, contra ETFs, sector mutual funds, countries, commodities, etc. Today, most sectors are covered by ETFs. For example, you do not need to buy gold coins to invest in that sector but the ETF GLD.

I am not a writer but a retail investor similar to most of my readers. I've been making a comfortable living via my investment ideas that I'm sharing in this book.

I have copied many ideas from my other books and have provided links to related articles in the internet for a more detailed discussion. "Sector Rotation in a Nutshell" should be read first. It helps you how to start to implement this strategy and serves as a frame work in using other features in this strategy such as favorable sectors in different phases of a market cycle and country sectors.

How this book is organized

This book has 12 sections covering most areas in sector rotation from my personal experience. It provides all the tools I know for successful practice of sector rotation.

Most graphs and tables are in landscape orientation (recommended for small screens) for both paperback and e-readers. Some graphs may not be displayed adequately on a small screen of an e-reader. E-readers may be available in the current version of Windows, so you can read e-books on the larger screen of your PC. For better orientation, just flip the e-readers 90 degrees. Some reader lets you select a table or a graph to display it to fit the screen.

A link is usually included for the most screens. Copy it to your browser to display the graphs on your PC if desirable. Instructions on how to produce some graphs are provided as you should try them out. One example is how to produce a chart on detecting market crashes.

The **font size** (Ctrl Minus for browser implementation of e-readers) and line spacing of most e-book formats can be adjusted. The unknown, special character is the "smiling face" that the current Kindle does not convert correctly as of this writing.

There are clickable links to web articles. Most of them are from my own web sites and public web sites such as Wikipedia. Some public links may not be available in the future as they are not under my control and my book offerings may change.

These links extend the usefulness of this book by making available specific topics that may not be interesting to every reader. It also provides articles (most are not written by me) for more in-depth analyzes.

Fidelity Video provides video clips to explain some basic terms and it may require Fidelity customers to sign on in order to view them. Check the trial offer from Fidelity. YouTube offers similar video lessons.

The current version provides most of the links the paperback readers can enter into your browser. Get the same information by entering a search in Wikipedia such as Dogs of Dow.

Investopedia is another source beside Wikipedia.
http://www.investopedia.com/

'Afterthoughts' includes my additional comments and ideas of minor importance. There are fillers with tips, refreshing pictures (taken by me) and jokes (most original) to fill up the empty space of the printed book. Fillers, links and afterthoughts may disrupt the flow of reading this book. However, no readers so far ask me to take them out even in the digitized version of this book. Many page breaks have been eliminated to improve the flow of the book.

For convenience, this book uses SPY, an Exchange Traded Fund (ETF) simulating the S&P 500, as the benchmark for the market. Annualized returns (Return * 365 / (Days between)) are used where appropriate for more meaningful comparison. To illustrate, I have a 10% return in 6 months, a 10% in a year and a 10% in 2 years. It is more meaningful to use annualized returns of 20%, 10% and 5% respectively for the 6-month return, the one-year return and the 2-year return in this example.

Usually I do not include the dividend, so you can add an estimated 1.5% to the annualized return. In addition, compound interest is not used for easier calculation, so the actual return could be even better.

About the author
I graduated from Cal. State University at San Jose in Industrial Engineering and University of Mass. in Amherst with a MS in

Industrial Engineering. I have retired from a job in IT. I have been an investor for over 30 years.

Dedication
To all retail investors and future retail investors including my grandchildren.

I sincerely hope this book will build bridges with fellow investors with different backgrounds.

Acknowledgement
Thanks to:
Poi for gathering my research info and working on the business side of the book.

Important Notice
© 2013-16 Tony Pow

Version	Paperback	Kindle
Edition 1	05/13	05/13
Edition 2	09/15	09/15
Edition 3	02/16	02/16
3.4	10/16	10/16

Disclaimer

Do not gamble money that you cannot afford to lose. Past performance is a guideline and is not necessarily indicative of future results. All information is believed to be accurate, but there it is not guaranteed. All the strategies including charts to detect market plunges described have no guarantee that they will make money and they may lose money. Do not trade without doing due diligence and be warned that most data would be obsolete. All my articles and the associated data are for informational and illustration purposes only. I'm not a professional investment counselor or a tax professional. Seek one before you make any investment decision. The above mentioned also applies for all other advice such as on accounting, taxes, health and any topic mentioned in this book. I am not a professional in any of these fields. Same for all the links contained in this book. Some articles may offend some one or some organization unintentionally. If I did, I'm sorry about that. I am politically and religiously neutral. I try my best effort to ensure the accuracy of my articles. Data also from different sources was believed to be accurate. However, there is no guarantee that they are accurate and suitable for the current market conditions and /or your individual situations. My publisher and I are not liable for any damages in using this book.

1   Highlights

Bubbles

Bubbles have existed throughout our history. Bubbles occur due to the excessive valuation driven up by the big institution investors (fund managers, pension managers, hedge fund manager, etc.). Asset valuations are then driven even higher by the retail investors. As of 3/2014, the market bubble is caused by the government stimulus by the injection of capital into the excessive money supply and subsidies. The first investors riding the wave make good money and the last ones buying at the peak will suffer most.

From our recent history, we have the 2000 internet bubble, and then the 2007 (2008 for some) housing bubble. The chapter Spotting Big Market Plunges illustrates it was easy to detect the last two plunges. Read the chapter AGAIN and digest it. It could save you more than 25% of your portfolio in the next plunge.

Today all the mentioned bubbles could be caused by pumping too much money into the economy by the government. However, the government cannot keep on injecting money into the economy and ask our children to pay our debts forever. When the injections stop, the market will drop fast and deep. As of 3/2014, the new Fed chairwoman most likely will not raise interest rate until the employment is lower than 6.5%. I estimate the interest rate will start to rise by the end of 2015 and the market / the economy will most likely be affected adversely.

3/2016 update
We have about 5% unemployment today. I expect the interest rate will be increased but in very small increments as the global economies are still poor.

USD

As of 1/2014, the gold price has been down from its height of 1,850. It will most likely remain in the range between 1,200 and 1,900 until the USD appreciates to the next level and / or the global economies improve. The USD is doing quite well recently (actually at its highest level since 2008). It could be the other countries (EU and Japan) are doing worse than us, as Einstein said, "everything is relative". The strong USD is not good for export and the global corporations would have less profit after converting back to USD. In addition, our shale energy is very promising, which will be clearer in two years whether it is just another mirage. [3/2016 Update: OPEC is dumping oil trying to drive the shale companies out of business.]

Bond

The bond bubble will burst when the interest rate rises. It will as the interest rate should be bottomed by now – it can't go negative I guess. I prefer to buy contra ETFs against 20-year Treasury bonds (TBF). Besides bonds, farm products and the farm land have reached high price levels. The student loan is getting its status as a bubble soon.

Stocks

There are several bubble stocks but they are few enough to move the entire market hopefully. From my technical indicators, the market is peaking and overbought as of 6/2014. Play defense with stop loss orders. So far I cannot find a potential trigger if the interest rate remains low. However, the record margin debt is a big concern. When the credit is tightened (due to higher interest rate), this bubble will burst. [3/2016 Update: It turns out the falling oil price drives the market down.]

What to act

Unless you ask me nicely to borrow my time machine which is still under development, you cannot pin point when the bubble will burst. Your timing to act depends on your risk tolerance, your knowledge (a commodity trader can afford to take more risk on commodities for example), your greed, and your past experience that could give you false security.

Today, we have the housing bubble (2007-2008), the gold bubble, the market bubble (2015), the second housing bubble, the debt bubble (2015), the bond bubble, the second market bubble, etc. It seems we can never get out the bubble cycle.

Since the world is economically connected better than before. When the USA sneezes, it affects our trading partners such as European countries, China and Japan, and also their partners such as the resource-rich countries in S. America, Australia, Russia, Canada and Africa.

For me, it is safer not to make the last buck as the reward / risk ratio is too low except on deeply-valued stocks. A good sleep would improve your health and that is worth all the gold in the world.

The power of market timing

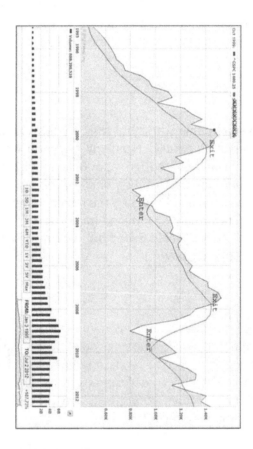

Detecting market plunges indicates the exit points and reentry points from 2000 to 9-2013 as follows. For simplicity, ignore the brief exits in 08/11/11 and after.

Table: Vital Dates

Market Plunge	Peak	Bottom	Indicator Exit	Indicator Reenter
2000	08/28/00	09/20/02	10/01/00	06/01/03
2007	10/12/07	03/06/09	02/01/08	09/01/09
			08/01/11	11/01/11

As of 04/2014, my chart (from Yahoo!Finance) still indicates to invest fully in the market. Run the simple chart once a month. When it indicates a potential market plunge is closer, run the chart once a week.

It is based on stock prices so it may not identify the peaks and bottoms precisely, but so far it has never failed to avoid big losses and ensure big gains by reentering the market. Hope it will give us enough time to act in the next market plunge as the last two did.

Unbelievable return with market timing

Calculate how much you made if you followed the above exit points and reenter points from 2000 to today. I bet you would make a good fortune.

To test the effect of market timing, I calculated the return of S&P 500 with market timing and compare it to the return of S&P 500 without market timing from 1-2000 to 9-2013.

There are many assumptions to make the calculations easier. In general, dividends are not considered. Compounding is not considered in most cases. The return with market timing should be substantially better if we buy a contra ETF during exits and sell it during reentries.

I was shocked by the incredible return by using simple market timing and the chart tells us to exit and reenter the market only 3 times from 2000 to 2013.

Summary info:

S&P 500	With Market Timing	Without Market

1-2000 to 9-2013		Timing
Better	**500%**	
Gain	1,000	167
Gain %	68%	11%
Annualized gained	5%	1%
Days	4,959	4,959

Calculations:

S & P 500	With Market Timing	Without Market Timing
1-2000	$1,469^1$	$1,469^1$
Exit 10/01/00	$1,041^2$	1,041
Enter 06/01/03	1,041	964^4
Exit 02/01/08	$1,489^3$	$1,379^4$
Enter 09/01/09	1489	$1,020^5$
Exit 08/01/11	1,888	1,293
Enter 11/01/11	1,888	1,251
09/03/13	2,469	1.638
Gained	2,469 – 1,469=1,000	1,638-1,469=167
Gain %	1000/1469 = 68%	167/1469 = 11%
Annualized gained	68% * 365/4959=5%	11%*365/4959=1%
Better	(1,000-167)/167 = 500%	

Portfolio with Market Timing:

[1] Both start with S&P 500 of 1,469 on 1-3-2000.

[2] 10/01/00.
The market timing portfolio exits the market and remains same value of 1,041 until 6/1/00.

[3]   02/01/08
The market timing portfolio exits the market and remains same value of 1,489 until 9/1/09.

1,489 is calculated as follows:
1,041 * (1 + Rate) = 1,041 * (1 + 1,379-964)/964) = 1,489
where S&P 500 is 964 on 6/1/00 and 1,379 on 2/1/08.

The other calculations are based on S&P 500 is 1,020 on 9/1/9, 1,293 on 8/1/11, 1,251 on 11/1/11 and 1,636 on 9/3/13.

Portfolio without Market Timing:

[1] Both starts with S&P 500 of 1,469 on 1-3-2000. We could use the 9/3/13 S&P 500 value, but it will not account on some compounded interest consideration.

[4] S&P 500 is 964 in 6/1/00 and 1,379 on 2/1/08.

[5] 02/01/08. The portfolio value is calculated to be 1,020 as follows:
1,379 * (1 + Rate) = 1,379 * (1 + (1020-1379)/1379) = 1,020
where S&P 500 is 1,379 on 2/1/08 and 1,020 on 9/1/09.

The other calculations are based on S&P 500 is 1,293 on 8/1/11, 1,251 on 11/1/11 and 1,636 on 9/3/13.

I cannot believe the shocking return with market timing. I checked my calculation and there was nothing wrong but do not hold me on this. Ignoring the compound rate of return should be minor. If you have time, send me your e-mail address to pow_tony@yahoo.com, so I can send you the spreadsheet to check out any error.

Even if I made a mistake somehow and got 100% instead of 500%, it still doubles the return without market timing! Ask any fund manager what it means to his or her fund performance and his / her career. It will detect the next market plunges, but it may not give us ample of time to react as the last two did. It will not detect the precise bottoms and peaks as they depend on the stock price of an ETF representing the market. I have separate statistics on market peaks and bottoms but they have not been proven. The above may not work as effectively if there are too many followers. On the contrary it may work as it could be a self-fulfilling prophesy.

The stock prices of SPY are obtained from Yahoo!Finance. The entry and exit points are obtained from my simple chart from Yahoo!Finance described and they are subject to my interpretation.

Afterthoughts

- Many including myself do not believe a market plunge is coming as of 7/2014. However, we have to be careful with the following analysis. Run the simple chart to spot any indication of a market plunge at least once a month.

  o Among my top-performing screens for the last 3 months, many top-performed screens are from the peak stage (defined by me) than other stages in a market cycle.

  o The typical market cycle is about 4 years. We have about 6 years since 2007.

  o The stock market has not reached the bubble stage yet. It will if it continues to rise at this pace in 2014.

- Some REITs are inversely affected by the rising interest rate. http://seekingalpha.com/article/1570772-american-capital-mortgage-investment-was-the-baby-thrown-out-with-the-bathwater

- Will the market go even higher as of 6/2014? We have to compare the risk / reward ratio. If the risk is too high, we may want to take some chips off the table.

- I was accused of selling the secrets of detecting market plunges for less than $10. My reply:

There are 4 groups of investors.
1. Institutional investors. Their performances vary. In short, hedge funds as a group do not beat the market in the last 5 years.
2. Mutual funds. Most cannot do market timing from their own regulations and as a group they do not beat the market after expenses.

3. Most retail investors who are always on the wrong side of the market via fears and greed.
4. While investors from #1 to #3 are losers, there must be some winners beating the market as a trade is a zero-sum game.

In theory, we cannot beat the mutual fund managers who have better resources. However, we can use market timing to our advantage.

Links

- DRIP. http://www.fool.com/dripport/whataredrips.htm

- A similar NYT article was posted about the same time by the famous Professor Krugman.
http://www.nytimes.com/2013/05/10/opinion/krugman-bernanke-blower-of-bubbles.html?_r=2&

- An article on "Why the author is shorting the market in mid 2013".
http://seekingalpha.com/article/1344071-5-reasons-why-i-am-shorting-the-market#comment_update_link

Megatrends

Every decade we have at least one megatrend: Natural resources in the 1970s, technology in 1990s, global companies whose services were needed by China during the last 30 years and so on. This decade we should have industries geared to the aging population such as health care and drugs.

I Strategy 1: Market Timing

"The Power of Market Timing" should convince you to rotate an ETF such as SPY and cash (or an ETF for short-term bonds) would give an incredible return. If you are aggressive, replace part of the cash with a contra ETF such as SH. All other strategies should follow this strategy. When the market tanks, most stocks will tank.

2   Simplest market timing

Market timing depends on charts; the following describes how to use chart information without creating charts. Most charts will not identify the peaks and bottoms of the market as they depend on data (i.e. the stock prices). However, it would reduce further loses.

It is simpler than it sounds. Just follow the following procedure.

How

The first part of this technique detects market plunges and the second part advises reentry to the market.

How to detect market plunges without charts (a.k.a. Death Cross)

1. Bring up Finviz.com.
2. Enter SPY (or any ETF that simulates the market).
3. If SMA-200% is positive, it indicates that market plunging has not been detected and you can skip the following steps.
4. The market is plunging if SMA-50% is more negative than SMA-200%. To illustrate this condition, SMA-200% is -2% and SMA-50% is -5%.
5. Sell most stocks starting with the riskiest ones first such as the ones with high P/Es and/or high Debt/Equity. Obtain this info from Finviz.com by entering the symbol of the stock you own.
6. For the conservative investors, sell those over-priced stocks only. For aggressive investors, sell all stocks. For the extreme aggressive ones, buy contra ETFs besides selling all stocks.

When to return to the market (a.k.a. Golden Cross)
Use the above in a reversed sense to detect whether the market has been recovering. However, when the SMA-200% is positive, I

would start buying value stocks (low P/E but the 'E' has to be positive and/or low Debt/Equity).

1. Bring up Finviz.com.
2. Enter SPY (or any ETF that simulates the market).
3. If SMA-200% is negative, the market is not recovering according to this indicator and you can skip the following steps.
4. Start buying the best value stocks. Sell all contra ETFs if you have any. You can re-evaluate the stocks from my list of my other book Best Stocks for 20XX. I should have a book when the market is favorable for buying stocks, but it is not a promise.
5. Market recovery is confirmed when SMA-50% is more positive than SMA-200%. To illustrate this condition, SMA-200% is 2% and SMA-50% is 5%. Commit larger percent (or all for aggressive investors) of your cash to stocks.

Do the above once a month. When the SPY price is closer to SMA actions percentage, perform the above once a week.

The charts and data for market timing described in this book are based on SMA-350 that is more preferred than this simple procedure without using charts.

Note. Predictions are predictions. However, the more the educated the guess is, the better chance the guess will materialize. It does not mean it will always materialize as the market changes and sometimes it is not rational.

My technical indicator (SMA-350) gave only one false alarm from 2000 to 2010. False signals happen more often after this period. The market is far more volatile than before. In most cases, false alarms will not hurt at all except the tax consequences on taxable accounts. The false alarm tells us to exit the market and come back to the market shortly.

3 Spotting big market plunges

This chapter is lengthy, complicated in some concepts and requiring you to try it yourself. Make your market decision by combining all the hints described in this article.

No one can consistently predict the correct stages of the market cycle. This chapter is intended for educational purpose only. However, if we have more rights than wrongs with our calculated and educated guesses, we should do well. As in everything in life, there is no guarantee.

There are my eight hints to identify a market plunge. The average loss of market plunges is about 45%. It could wipe out most gains for the entire market cycle. We target to avoid half of the loss.

Do not buy stocks during market plunge that could last for more than a year, which is defined by me from the market peak to the market bottom.

Eight hints of a market plunge

1. Technical analysis (TA).

    The following chart is created by Yahoo!Finance. If it does not display well on a small screen, copy the following link to your browser to display it on your PC.
    http://ebmyth.blogspot.com/2013/05/ta-graph-for-spotting-plunges-chapter.html

    ---

    It can be created by following the steps; you need to create one yourself to detect the next plunge with current data.
    *   From Yahoo!Finance or any chart systems, enter SPY (or S&P 500 index) or an ETF that represents the total market.
    *   Select Interactive Chart.
    *   Click Technical Indicators.
    *   Select SMA (simple moving average).
    *   Enter 350 days (actually it is trade sessions). Many chart systems use 'month' as unit, enter 12 or 11.67 if decimals is allowed (=350/12) instead of 350.

- Enter 1-3-2000 on "FROM:" or any "from date" that fits your screen.
- Select Draw.
- Note. I switch to Fidelity for charting now as I cannot produce the same info from Yahoo!Finance. It could be my fault or a bug that should be fixed.

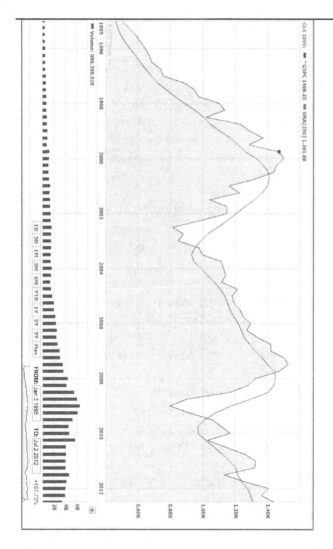

350 days simple moving average (SMA). Yahoo!Finance

The red line is the 350-day SMA, Simple Moving Average. If the stock price is below the moving average, it has detected a market plunge by this chart. Return to the market when the price is above the moving average line described as Early Recovery later. "350 days" are trading sessions. I have tried different "days" and 350 is the best fit for the last two market plunges, but it does not mean it would be the best fit the next market plunge.

We have two cycles described in the chart. From the above, we should leave the market in the first quarter of 2000 and return to the market on the first quarter of 2003.

On the second cycle, the chart tells us to get out in Dec. 2008 and come back in July 2009 approximately. Enlarge the chart by selecting 5 years instead of the maximum or use a larger monitor for a more detailed chart. The chart sometimes gives false signals to tell us to exit but tell us to reenter briefly. In most cases, we do not lose much except the tax consequences for selling. No technical indicators are perfect.

I started to come back on Feb. 2009. It was perfect timing but most likely or partly it was due to good luck. I was partially influenced by several articles I read.

Technical Analysis is based on the past data, so you cannot avoid the initial losses but it could reduce further and larger losses. From the above, the chart detected the two big plunges nicely allowing enough time to take actions. Will the next plunge be detected? It will I guess. However, it may not allow enough time as the last two.

Sometimes, we time it wrongly or prematurely and miss some gains by leaving the market too early. We need to treat it as buying insurance; it only pays big when the worst happens. When the "reward / risk" is too low, it is better to stay in cash. One's opinion.

Return to equity when the price is above the moving average (the red line). You should profit more by following the chart than 'Buy and Hold' or keeping your money under the pillow. For the last two market cycles, I returned to equities in Early Recovery (a stage of the market cycle defined by me) and profited. Can I be 100% sure for the next market plunge and come back in a timely order? Certainly not.

If most of your stocks are in tech, use QQQ instead of SPY. In addition QQQ is more volatile than SPY and the tech sector usually leads the market.

Other technical indicators:

- Header and Shoulder would predict a market plunge as evidenced in 2007. The reverse pattern would predict a market surge as indicated in 2009.
- Double Top is a bearish signal and double bottom is a bullish signal.
- Death Cross is used to detect marge plunges and it does not require charting via finviz.com. Golden Cross detects when to return.
- MACD (Moving Average Convergence Divergence). When the indicator is below the zero line, it is bearish and vice versa. Use it as a secondary indicator to detect the market direction.
- When RSI (14) is over 65%, the market is most likely overbought (i.e. over-valued).
- Use the following SMA-20 as a secondary indicator as an alternative to the SMA-350. When the stock price is below SMA-20 (Single Moving Average for the last 20 sessions) for the consecutive 3 days, it indicates a possible market plunge. In theory, the institution investors dump the stock on the first day and then the retail investors follow on the second day. If it continues on the third day, most likely it is not the trick of the institution investors to take advantage of the retail investors.

2. Do the opposite of the flow of the dumb money.

When everyone is buying recklessly, making money and proclaiming that they are geniuses, sell. In 1999, my friend told me that he should quit his job and concentrate on investing as he was making many times in the stock market over his regular salary by spending half an hour a day. I would call myself a genius by making $1,000 an hour. When AAII's bullish sentiment (a contrary indicator to me) is over 70%, watch out.

On the same year, there were so many successful IPOs with '.com' names and these companies did not know how to make profits but blindly captured their market shares at all expenses.

They gave me $20 for just registering in their site. The poor quality of their ads showing their products during the Super Bowl reflected the quality of their management. The so-called 'MBA's business model' of capturing a potential market of one million potential sales by spending five millions is not Business 101 but Fool 101.

The inverse flow of money market funds is a good indicator too. The more money flowing into the equity funds by retail investors, the riskier is the market. Greed is a human nature. It is hard to resist buying stocks when your friends are all making good money in the market and you feel you do not want to miss the boat. I tried unsuccessfully to convince lottery winners not buying lottery and they showed me they had made another thousands yesterday.

Fear and Greed index from cnnFn.com is a similar contrary index. Leave the market when Greed is high and vice versa.

Many high-flying internet stocks lost more than 95% of their peak values. As in any bubble, the last ones to get into the bubble suffer most. The investors make out pretty nicely if they use the strategies below:
- Use stop loss to protect the profits. Adjust the order when the stock appreciates.
- Use SMA-20% (from Finviz.com). When the stock falls below Simple Moving Average for the last 20 sessions, sell it. Use SMA-50 instead if you have higher risk tolerance.

3. Duration.
Cycles usually occur every four or five years. This is a very rough estimate as cycles often vary from 1 to 8 or even more years. The market plunge in 2007-2008 proceeded one of the longest market cycles. The longer it stays at the peak, the higher the chance the market will plunge and the further it will sink. I call it Newton's Law of Gravity or 'What goes up must come down'.

4. Valuation.
The average historical P/E of the S&P 500 is about 15. When it is over the average, be careful. Obtain the P/E of SPY (an ETF for the

S&P 500) from Yahoo!Finance and confirm it in many other sources. When the average P/E of a sector is over 35, most likely there will be a fierce correction for that sector. When it is over 40, the market most likely has peaked. When you find fewer value stocks than before, it means the market is more risky now.

The P/E of S&P 500 was 28 in 2000. It was 18 in 2007 and 16 in 2015. Both are over 15, the average value for the last five years.

The value of the average P/E has to be adjusted as the market conditions are not the same 10 or so years ago. Today (2016) part of the earning (the E in P/E) is due to the low cost in borrowing and less wage cost due to hiring overseas. Most global corporations can offshore jobs to reduce expenses. The global economies are inter-connected far better than before. When the global economies fall, we will fall too.

Other related hints on value:

The oil and industrial commodities (copper, steel...) are within 20% of their record highs. From my memory, it is the first time that oil is in sync with the market due to the dumping of stocks by the oil-producing countries today.

The total market cap is higher than the GDP. As of Nov., 2013, "Market Cap / GDP" is about 110% (fair at 85%) and hence it is over-valued. Daily ratios can be obtained from GuruFocus.com, a paid subscription service. It does not work in the current cycle from 2008. It may be today due to most large companies are multi-national. However, today most large companies are global companies, so it loses some luster in using this ratio.

From my observation, the higher the interest rate is, the higher the chance for a market plunge will be. The companies will have less earnings due to the higher borrowing costs especially in businesses that require a lot of borrowing and/or most of their customers' purchases are via financing. The stocks are more expensive to buy using margin accounts. Hence, the market will not fare well when the Fed hikes the interest rate.

Q including intangible assets is with P/E in evaluating the value of the market. It is harder to calculate.

Shiller P/E (same as CAPE or PE10)

It can be used to detect the valuation of the market. The P is the S&P500 (or use SPY) and E is the average earnings of last 10 years. It can also be used on sector ETFs and stocks. Use it as one of the hints. The major flaw is 10 years is too long a time.

To simplify, most likely the market valuation is low (good to buy) when the P/E is below 15. The market valuation is high when it is above 20. As of 2014, it is far above 20 (17 in 2/2016). CAPE (cyclically adjusted price/earnings ratio) is available from the web by searching "CAPE P/E" to get the current reading.

Shiller's P/E http://www.gurufocus.com/shiller-PE.php
His 2014 call, Second link

From the above links, CAPE has been pretty decent. The reason why it does not work in 2014 is the excessive money printing that makes the market not rational. Treat it as a secondary yardstick.

5. Triggers to burst a bubble.

In 2000, the trigger was the tech bubble. In 2007 it was the housing (or financing) bubble. It was easy to spot a massive tech bubble in 2000. I moved most of my tech sector funds to traditional sectors (cash for 20-20 hindsight) in the beginning of April, 2000, which was too close for comfort to this market plunge.

Most investors including myself did not understand the workings of the derivatives of the mortgage loans and could not recognize the bubble. I made good money in the oil sector in 2007. However, in 2008 most of my investments were losers including the investment in the oil sector. If I followed the hints described in this chapter, I would have avoided heavy losses.

6. Rising interest rate.

It is more expensive for investors using margin to buy stocks, for companies to borrow money and for consumers to buy high ticket items and houses.

A related hint is rising margin debt (the debt used to buy stocks backed up by the current stock holdings). When we have a record margin debt as in 2016, the chance of a market plunge is high when the Fed hikes the interest rate.

When the Fed discount rate is 5% or above, be careful. This is also the time to buy long-term bonds. When it is 1% or less, most likely the market starts to recover. This is also the time NOT to buy long-term bonds. This strategy was proven in market cycles in 2000 and 2008.

7. Yield Curve.

When the short-term (say 3 month) interest rate is higher than the long term (say 30 years), it is abnormal and a bearish signal. Click here to check the yield curve.

http://www.treasury.gov/resource-center/data-chart-center/interest-rates/Pages/TextView.aspx?data=yield

http://blogs.marketwatch.com/thetell/2014/05/13/bear-market-wont-come-until-the-yield-curve-says-so-kleintop/

8. Rising oil price.

It is the same as the above as rising oil price will cause everything more expensive. However, today (2015-2016) is an exception. The falling oil price correlates with the market. It is due to falling too much and the oil-producing countries have to dump the stocks to rescue their economies.

Be conservative

As in any new strategy, test it out and try it out gradually with real money. Most of you paid less than $25 for this book and most likely you do not want to risk all your money based on a $25 advice, so consult your financial advisors.

You should not lose money by existing the market too early, but miss the opportunity to make more money. If the market does not crash, treat it as insurance.

The chart worked fine for the last two crashes, but as in life there is no guarantee to detect the next market crash for the following reasons:

- It may not give us ample of time to react as the last two. The current market is high and is caused by excessive money supply. When the money supply is reduced (or no more QEn), the market will react negatively.

- When too many folks buy my books and use the same chart, it will lose its effectiveness. It is most likely not, but there is always a chance.

- Past performances do not guarantee future performance.

- The market is not always rational.

- There are more noises (crossing the red line and backing again briefly) since 2011. The chart is not the only indicator I follow. Adjust it according to your risk tolerance.

  However, if you follow the chart, you're doing quite well since 2000. From 2000 to 2010, we only have 3 exits/entries and one is very brief.

  Since 2011, there are several exits/entries as the market is not rational. However, if you follow it, you're still faring well as they tell you reentry very quickly. You do not lose or gain a lot by doing so. Even if you lose a little, it could be the best insurance you bought.

  The noises would be increased if we use 200 days in SMA in the chart instead of 350. For the same reason, they will be decreased if I use 400 days but the signal will be later delayed.

  As in life, there is nothing guaranteed, the chart is far better than market timing without charts and/or no market timing at all since 2000. As of 6/2015, I started looking at my charts more frequently months as we've been living dangerously on borrowed time for a long while.

Conclusion

This article provides my basic tools and my views on market timing. Market is not always rational otherwise there are no poor folks as stated before. When the market is about to plunge, run the chart more frequently and read more articles written by market experts.

Market timing is not an exact science but it is based on educated guesses. The better guesses should have more rights than wrongs in the long term. Your actions depend on your risk tolerance. Initially you should be careful on using any strategy that you do not have full understanding and enough proven record.

Afterthoughts

- The 350 in SMA-350 is the number of the last trade sessions instead of calendar days. I have tried 200 and many other days and found 350 is the best fit for detecting market plunges.

  SMA-200 is faster than SMA-350 but it gives more false signal to leave the market. The confirmations of a market plunge are: 1. SMA-200% is 5 or more negative and 2. SMA-20 and SMA-50 are also negative.

  I find SMA-200 is a better signal to reenter the market for the last two plunges.

  Most beginners commit a serious mistake in learning too many indicators for market timing. Besides SMA, RSI is the one you should know. Other indicators are good for confirmation only.

- I have many critiques telling me no one can predict market plunges. They have not read this article. After you read this chapter, I hope you at least agree that we can reduce a lot of losses just by following the simple chart.

- It is funny that I was accused of selling my 'secret' of market timing for less than $10. This is the most-kept secret. I 'discovered' it by accident and tried many combinations to find the best day for the moving average for the last two plunges. I found it is 350 days. It is so simple that I believe many have discovered it but no one wants to share it. I tried 200 days before but it seems giving signals too early.

- You have to be cautious and only you are responsible for your actions in investing. From the last two plunges, the chart is great in predicting plunges. Most likely it will detect the next one but I'm not sure whether we have ample of time to prepare as the last two did.

  Exiting the market too early or entering the market too late would lose some profit potential. As long as you do not sell short (not recommended) and / or buy contra ETFs (risky), you do not lose any of your money.

  However, if the market crashes too fast (it is possible today as the market has been extremely high as of 2015), then the indicator would show us far too late to react. When the market is risky (close to the crossing), check the charts more frequently. In any case, it is still better than 'buy-and-hold' strategy.

- After the early recovery in 2009, we had a temporary market top in 4/2012. Click here for the blog on a good prediction of the temporary market top. Read the comments on the updates. Again, I hope to achieve more right predictions than the wrong ones and it is just a prediction. Check out my logic so it may be useful in the future with similar market conditions. This was a correction (i.e. a temporary market top) and it was not the market peak. Corrections happen on the average two times a year.

  (http://tonyp4idea.blogspot.com/2012/04/market-top.html)

- When the increase of the market disproportionally larger than that of GDP, a bubble is forming. Same for company when its stock price increases disproportionally from its earnings.

- The financial collapse of 2007 was caused by easy credit, fraudulent credit applications, greed, poor regulations / enforcement... It led to the collapse of derivatives. Have we learned the lessons so not to repeat them again?

  1. Many banks were bailed out. Many CEOs were rewarded with 'bonuses'. Even the CEO of Lehman Brothers got away with good loots. No one goes to jail so far.
  2. The products based on derivatives were rated AAA by the rating agencies. How many have been prosecuted? What have the law makers done to regulate our financial system?
  3. Many pension funds lost big money. If the smartest guys do not fare well, why should we the retail investors still invest in investments we do not understand?
  4. Some governments such as Hong Kong cannot prosecute the bankrupted Lehman Brothers, but they punish the banks that sold these derivative products disguised as safe 'mini bonds'.

- High Low Index spot market plunges / corrections.
(http://www.marketwatch.com/story/sell-signal-from-key-market-indicator-2013-07-17?dist=beforebell)

  "The indicator represents the lesser of two numbers: New 52-week highs and new 52-week lows (both expressed as a percentage of total issues traded). High readings are bearish, while low levels are bullish."

  "Fosback recommended using a 10-week exponential moving average of the weekly values. When that average reached 5%, he said it indicated "extreme market divergence" and therefore bearish. And that's just what the indicator did in June, rising to 5.1%. It currently stands at 4.6%." Try it out using Yahoo!Finance. Enter SPY or any ETF that represents the market. Select Interactive Chart, Exponential Moving Average and 10 weeks or 70 days.

- Future market direction is a contrarian-sentiment measured by put/call option volume ratio. A volume of too many put buyers usually signals that a market bottom is coming, while too many call buyers typically indicates a market top is close.

- Read the current opinions from the experts. Start with the Macro View of SeekingAlpha, MarketWatch and CNNfn. Wall Street Journal and Barron's are usually more conservative and written by experts. Usually there are two camps: for and against a market crash. Digest them and decide the market direction by yourself.

- Misc. prediction indicators using SPY (from Yahoo!Finance & mulpl.com).
  - P/S (Price / Sale) > 1.7.
  - Less than 50 of S&P 500 hit new high.
  - Advance/Decline < 1 for over 3 months.
  - Reversing indicators of the above, such as P/S > 1.5 and the market is still rising.
  - AAII bearish less than 20% from an average of about 30%, a contrary indicator.
  - Using Finviz.com, when SMA50% is higher than SMA200%, most likely we're in a bull market. Similar if consumer discretionary sector is rising.

II Strategy 2: Rotation of 4 Sectors

Rotate sectors via ETFs and/or mutual funds. When the market is risky (Chapter 2), move them to cash, short-term bond ETF/mutual fund, money market fund or a combination of the above and reenter when the market is not risky.

4   Rotation of 4 ETFs

Evaluate an ETF

ETF is a basket of stocks according to a specific sector, country or a theme.

From Yahoo!Finance, enter the symbol of the ETF such as XLU. It displays its historical P/E (last twelve months). If it is below 15 and above zero, it could be a value ETF. Also, if the current price is lower than its NAV, it is sold with discount (or premium vice versa). Compare its YTD Return to SPY's.

From Finviz.com, enter the ETF symbol. If SMA-20%, SMA-50% and SMA-200% are all positive, most likely the ETF is in uptrend. To illustrate, SMA-200 is Simple Moving Average for the last 200 trade sessions (no trading on weekends and specific holidays). The percent is how much the stock price of the ETF above the SMA. If the percent is negative, it means the stock price is below the SMA.

If your average holding period is about 50 days, SMA-50% is more appropriate to you for example.

If RSI(14) > 70, it is probably over-sold; if it is < 35, it is probably under-sold (i.e. value).

In addition, ensure the average volume is high (more than 10,000 shares to me), market cap is more than 200 M, and it has low fee. Most popular ETFs have these characteristics. Avoid leveraged ETFs for now.

How to determine the sector has been recovered

It is easier to profit by following the uptrend of an ETF using the above info. It is hard to detect when the bottom of an ETF has been reached. If SMA-20%, SMA-50% and SMA-200% are all positive, most likely the ETF is in uptrend or it has recovered. It does not always happen as predicted, so use stops to protect your investment.

An example

This example illustrates how to evaluate ETFs. First, determine whether the market is risky. Most beginners should not invest in a risky market. Advance investors can bet against the market or a specific sector by buying contra ETFs or puts.

Next, you want to limit the number of sector ETFs by selecting those that are either trending up or hitting bottom (bottom is harder to predict). Personally I prefer sectors with long-term uptrend (indicated by cnnfn.com). Seeking Alpha has many current articles on ETFs.

Today's market (as of 2/5/2016) is risky. For illustration only, I select the following ETFs: SPY (simulating the market based on large companies), XLP (consumer staples) and XLY (consumer discretionary). XLP should perform better than XLY during a recession as those products are the necessities.

Technical indicators such as SMA-50 (Simple Moving Average for the last 50 sessions), SMA-200 and RSI(14) are from finviz.com and the rest are from Yahoo!Finance.com. After you buy the ETF, use stop loss to protect your investment. Bio tech sector moved up for many months until it crashed later in 2015.

As of 2/5/2016	SPY	XLP (staples)	XLY (discret.)
Price	190	50	71
NAV	192	50	73
• Technical			
SMA-50	-4%	0%	-7%
SMA-200	-6%	2%	-7%
RSI(14)	44	50	36
Other	Double bottom at $186		

• Fundamental			
P/E	17	20	19
Yield	2.1%	2.5%	1.5%
YTD return	-5%	0.5%	-5%
Net asset	174 B	9 B	10 B

Explanation

- The figures may not be identical from the two web sites due to the dates they use.
- XLY has better discount among the 3 ETFs as most investors believe a recession is coming.
- XLP has less down trend among the 3 ETFs as expected.
- XLY is more undersold among the 3 as expected.
- Double bottom is a technical pattern that indicates the stock would surge.
- SPY has better valued according to its P/E.
- XLY's dividend is the least among the 3 as they have more tech companies in the ETF. They have to plow back the profits to research and development.
- XLP has the best YTD return among the 3.
- As long as the asset is above 500 M (200 M for specialized ETFs), it is fine and all three pass this mark.

There are many metrics such as Debt/Equity not available from these two web sites. Many sites list the top holding of a specific ETF. Just average the metrics of the top ten or so of its stock holdings.

Filler:

Poor Lochte

Lochte was born in the wrong time and wrong place. Without Phelps he could make top money in endorsements. Now, they are all gone for making a simple lie on a very minor situation. He is NOT a role model anymore! That's what happened when the family (most likely) did not give him a decent education on honesty and be careful on drinks and drugs. It will not be the last time as we're in a permissive culture. All the politicians think they can fool us all the time and they should learn it from Lochte.

III Strategy 3: Rotation of more sectors

It is similar to the Strategy 2 but includes more basic sectors. Add a contra ETF such as SH to take advantage of a falling market. Add the following sector ETFs to the four sectors described in Strategy 2: XLY, XLP, XLE, XLF, XLU, IYW, XHB, IYM, OIL and XLU. They should cover most of the sectors.

Start keeping the top two sectors to start. The allocation percentages depend on individual risk tolerance. You can use indexed mutual funds. Compare their expenses and restrictions.

Select the best performer of last month. Besides cnnfn.com and finviz.com, the current, favorable sectors can be found in many web sites including SeekingAlpha.com and Fidelity.com (customers only). Following the top performer(s) for the last month is following the short-term trend. In addition to the last month, following the top performer(s) for the last 3 months is following the trend for the intermediate trend.

As of Feb., 2016, the utility index within S&P 500 has been up about 8% year-to-date while S&P 500 was down by about 8%. It is another example that the correct sector rotation is profitable.

The primary sectors are: Basic Materials, Consumer Discretionary, Consumer Staples, Energy, Financial, Health Care, Industrial, Technology and Utilities. Click the links or search from Wikipedia for description of these sectors.

https://www.fidelity.com/sector-investing/overview

We can sub divide a sector into industries. For example, Technology can be divided into Computer and Software. When computer industry is good, it does not mean software industry is also good. Some industries such as banking software can cross more than one sector.

The above links describe sectors pretty good by Fidelity with the exception of Technology, which is divided into several sectors such as Software, Computer and Telecom by Fidelity. Here are my views on the major sectors. Many vendors including IBD provide industry rankings. Here is my additional description to cover the basic sectors and some will be described in the appropriate chapters.

Consumer Staples and Discretionary

Consumer Staples are food, beverages, household products and the products we buy as necessity. They are recession-proof. The US products have demonstrated high quality and safety. With the growing middle class in developing countries such as China and India, we expect they should grow outside the USA. Currently it is not due to tariffs.

Consumer Discretionary are just the opposite.

Besides introducing the sectors and their corresponding mutual funds and ETFs, I introduce how to evaluate sectors fundamentally and technically. For beginners, skip the rest of this section.

Links

A list of sectors.
http://www.investorguide.com/sector-list.php
Check's sector analysis.
http://seekingalpha.com/article/2806655-the-stock-market-2015-a-sector-by-sector-valuation-perspective-part-1-an-overview

Filler:

The fisherman and the sea

The smart fisherman (investor) would not venture out (buy stocks) to the stormy sea (the risky market) according to the weather forecast (technical indicator).

Recently I evaluated 10 stocks. The best return is GPRO about 10% up in two or three weeks but the rest are losers. I prefer to rise with the tide.

5   ETFs / Mutual Funds

What is an ETF

Fidelity: Index ETFs (https://www.fidelity.com/etfs/overview).

Wikipedia on ETF (http://en.wikipedia.org/wiki/Exchange-traded_fund).

List of ETFs
ETF Bloomberg
http://www.bloomberg.com/markets/etfs/
ETF data base
http://etfdb.com/
ETF Trends
http://www.etftrends.com/
A list of ETFs. Seeking Alpha.
(http://etf.stock-encyclopedia.com/category/)

Fidelity's commission-free ETFs. Check current offering and whether they are still commission-free.
(https://www.fidelity.com/etfs/ishares)

Fidelity Annuity funds with performance data.
http://fundresearch.fidelity.com/annuities/category-performance-annual-total-returns-quarterly/FPRAI?refann=005

A list of contra ETFs (or bear ETFs)
http://www.tradermike.net/inverse-short-etfs-bearish-etf-funds/

Misc.: ETFGuide, ETFReplay (highly recommended).

Other resources
Your broker should have a lot of information on ETFs and many offer commission-free ETFs.

Most subscription services offer research on ETFs. IBD has a strategy dedicated to ETFs and so is AAII to name a couple.

Seeking Alpha has extensive resources for ETF including an ETF screener and investing ideas.

Not all ETFs are created equal
Check their performances and their expenses.

Small but well-performed ETFs
Here is a list.
http://finance.yahoo.com/news/small-etfs-pack-big-punch-195430875.html

Guggenheim Spin-Off ETF (CSD) looks interesting. The ETF tracks corporate spinoffs. It has beaten SPY for a long while; check the current performance. Not a recommendation.

When not to use ETFs
I prefer sector mutual funds in some industries that need to extensive research. They are drug industry, banks, miners and insurers.

Half ETF
Taking out half of the stocks that score below the average in an index ETF could beat the same full ETF itself. I call it HETF (half the ETF). You hear it here first. I hope all the fund creators of HETF (trademark pending ☺) will donate to my secret retiring fund for using the name and my concept.

To illustrate, sort the expected P/E (not including stocks with negative earnings) in ascending order and only include the stocks on the first half. Add more fundamental metrics. It will take minutes.

Disadvantages of ETFs

- When you have two stocks in a sector ETF one good one and one bad one, the ETF treats them the same. Stock pickers would buy the one with better appreciation potential.
- The return is better than the actual return due to stock rotation. To illustrate, on August 29, 2012, SHLD was replaced by LYB in a sector fund. SHLD was down by 4% and LYB was up by 4% primarily due to the switch. Unless you sell and buy at the right time (that's impossible), your return would not match with the ETF's return due to the replacement.

- Ensure the performance matches the corresponding index, which is most likely does not include dividends.

Advantages of ETFs

- We have demonstrated you can beat the market by using market timing. Between 2000 and Nov., 2013, you only exit and reenter the market 3 times and the result is astonishing.
- It is easy to rotate a sector vs. buying/selling all stocks in this sector. It makes sector rotation the same as trading a stock.
- The risk is spread out and your portfolio is diversified especially for a market ETF or buying three or more ETFs in different sectors.
- Eliminate the time in researching stocks.

Leveraged ETFs

I do not recommend them. Some are 2x, 3x and even higher. They're too risky. However, when you are very sure or your strategy has very low drawdown, you may want to use them to improve performance. I recommend skipping all leveraged ETFs.

My basic ETF tables

I use a list of selected ETFs and commission-free (check details) ETFs from Fidelity for my purpose. I include some mutual funds and mutual funds for Fidelity's annuity. Some may be interesting to you. I use ETFs for sector rotation and parking my cash when the market is favorable and I do not have stocks I want to buy.

ETFs and funds come and go. Some ideas and classifications are my interpretation.

Table by market cap:

Category	ETF	Fidelity ETF	Mutual Funds	Fidelity's Annuity	Contra ETF
Size:					
Large Cap	DOW		See Blend		DOG
	SPY				SH
	QQQ	ONEQ			PSQ

	RYH				
Blend	IWD	IVV	BEQGX		
Growth	SPYG	IVW	FBGRX		
Value	SPYV		DOGGX		
Dividend	NOBL	DVY	FRDPX		
	VYM				
Mid Cap				FNBSC	MYY
Blend	MDY	JJH	VSEQX		
Growth		IJK	STDIX		
			BPTRX		
Value		IJJ	FSMVX		
Small Cap				FPRGC	SBB
Blend	IWM	IJR	HDPSX		
Growth		IJT	PRDSX		
Value		IJS	SKSEX		
Micro	IWC				
Multi					
Blend			VDEOX		
Growth			VHCOX		
Value			TCLCX		
Bond					
Long Term (20)	VLV		BTTTX		TBF
Mid Term (7 – 10)	VCIT		FSTGX		
Short Term (1 – 3 yrs.)	VCSH		THOPX		
Total	BOND		PONDX		
Corp Invest Grade	VCIT		NTHEX		
High Yield (junk)	PHB		SPHIX		
Muni	MUB		Check state		
Special situation					
Buy back	PKW				

Table by sectors:

Sector	ETF	Fidelity ETF	Mutual Funds	Fidelity's Annuity
Banking[1]			FSRBK	
Regional	IAT			
Bio	IBB		FBIOX	
	XBI		Large	
Consumer Dis.	XLY	FDIS	FSCPX	FVHAC
Consumer Staple	XLP	FSTA	FDFAX	FCSAC
Finance	KIE	FNCL	FIDSX	FONNC
	IYF			
Energy	XLE	FENY	FSENX	FJLLC
Energy Service			FSESX	
Gold	GLD		FSAGX	
Gold Miner	GDX		VGPMX	
Health Care	IYH	FHLC	FSPHX	FPDRC
	VHT		VGHCX	
House Builder	ITB		FSHOX	
	ITB		Perform	
Industrial	IYJ	FIDU	FCYIX	FBALC
Material	VAW	FMAT	FSDPX	
	IYM			
Oil	USO			
Oil Service	OIH		FSESX	
Oil Exploration	XOP			
Real Estate	VNQ		FRIFX	FFWLC
REIT	VNQ			
Retail	RTH		FSRPX	
	XRT			
Regional bank	KRE		FSRBX	
Semi Conduct	SMH			
Software	XSW		FSCSX	
	IGV			
Technology	XLK	FTEC	FSPTX	FYENC
	FDN		FBSOX	
			ROGSX	
Telecomm.	VOX	FCOM	FSTCX	FVTAC
Transport	XTN			

	IYT			
Utilities	XLU	FUTY	FSUTX	FKMSC
Wireless			FWRLX	

Footnote. [1] Also check Finance.

Table by countries:

Country	ETF	Fidelity ETF	Mutual Funds	Fidelity's Annuity
Australia	EWA			
Brazil	EWZ			
Canada	EWC		FICDX	
China	FXI		FHKCX	
EAFE	EFA			
Emerging	VWO		FEMEX	FEMAC
Europe	VGK		FIEUX	
Global	KXI		PGVFX	
Greece	GREK			
India	INDY		MINDX	
Indonesia	EIDO			
Latin America	ILF		FLATX	
Nordic			FNORX	
Hong Kong	EWH			
Japan	EWJ		FJPNX	
S. Africa	EZA			
S. Korea	EWY		MAKOX	
Singapore	EWS			
Taiwan	EWT			
Turkey	TUR			
United Kingdom	EWU			
Foreign:				
Combination	1	2	3	4
Intern. Div.	IDV	DWX		
Small Cap	SCZ	GWX		
Value	EFV			
Europe	VGK			

6   Quick analysis of ETFs

Evaluate an ETF

ETF is a basket of stocks according to a specific sector, country or a theme. I use different yardsticks to evaluate ETFs.

From Yahoo!Finance, enter the symbol of the ETF. It displays its historical P/E (last twelve months). If it is below 15 and above zero, it could be valued. Also, if the current price is lower than its NAV, it is sold with discount (or premium vice versa). Compare its YTD Return to SPY's.

From Finviz.com, enter the ETF symbol. If SMA-20%, SMA-50% and SMA-200% are all positive, most likely the ETF is in uptrend. If your average holding period is about 50 days, SMA-50% is more meaningful to you. If RSI(14) > 70, it is probably over-sold; if it is < 35, it is probably under-sold (i.e. value).

In addition, ensure the average volume is high (more than 10,000 shares to me), market cap is more than 200 M, and it has low fee... Most popular ETFs have these characteristics.

How to determine the sector has been recovered

It is easier to profit by following the uptrend (or downtrend for shorting and/or contra ETFs) of an ETF using the above info. It is hard to detect when the bottom of an ETF has been reached. If SMA-20%, SMA-50% and SMA-200% are all positive, most likely the ETF is in uptrend or it has recovered. It did not happen for some ETFs in 2015.

An example

This example illustrates how to evaluate ETFs. First, determine whether the market is risky. If it is risky and you're more risk tolerant, you can buy contra ETF(s) betting the market or the specific sector will go further down. Most investors should not invest in a risky market.

Next, you want to limit the number of sector ETFs by selecting those that are either trending up or hitting bottom. Personally I prefer sectors with long-term uptrend (indicated by cnnfn.com). Seeking Alpha has many current articles on ETFs.

Today's market (as of 2/5/2015) is risky. For illustration only, I select the following ETFs: SPY (simulating the market based on large companies), XLP (consumer staples) and XLY (consumer discretionary). XLP should perform better than XLY during a recession as those products are the necessities.

Technical indicators such as SMA-50 (Simple Moving Average for the last 50 sessions), SMA-200 and RSI(14) are from finviz.com and the rest are from Yahoo!Finance.com. After you buy the ETF, use stop loss to protect your investment. Bio tech sector moved up for many months until it crashed later in 2015.

As of 2/5/2015	SPY	XLP (staples)	XLY (discret.)
Price	190	50	71
NAV	192	50	73
• Technical			
SMA-50	-4%	0%	-7%
SMA-200	-6%	2%	-7%
RSI(14)	44	50	36
Other	Double bottom at $186		
• Fundamental			
P/E	17	20	19
Yield	2.1%	2.5%	1.5%
YTD return	-5%	0.5%	-5%
Net asset	174 B	9 B	10 B

Explanation

- The figures may not be the same from the two web sites due to the date they use.
- XLY has better discount among the 3 ETFs as most investors believe a recession is coming.
- XLP is less down trend among the 3 ETFs as expected.
- XLY is more undersold among the 3 as expected.
- Double bottom is a technical pattern that indicates the stock would surge.

- SPY has better valued according to P/E.
- XLY's dividend is the least among the 3 as they have more tech companies. They have to plow back the profits to research and development.
- XLP has the best YTD return among the 3.
- As long as the asset is above 500 M, it is fine and all three pass this mark.

There are many metrics such as Debt/Equity not available from the two web sites. Many sites list the top holding of a specific ETF. Just average the metrics of the top ten or so of its holdings.

Picture filler: Who beautifies the other?

7   Sectors to be cautious

There are many reasons to be very cautious when investing in the following sectors. However, Technical Analysis (a.k.a. charting) would give you more hints than the fundamentals for stocks in these sectors. The following sectors should be cautious.

Loan companies/banks

The financial statements do not show the quality of their loan portfolios. Following this advice, you may be able to skip the banks that melt down in 2007. The peak of Citigroup is $550 and several banks bankrupted.

Drug (generic is ok)

Understanding the complexities of the drug pipelines, its potential profits for new drugs and the expiration of its current drugs may not be worth the effort for most retail investors. In addition, a serious lawsuit and / or a serious problem of a drug could wipe out a good percentage of the stock price. When a drug shows unpromising sign(s) in any trial phase, the stock could plunge and vice versa.

Miners

It is extremely difficult to estimate how much ore (sometimes a miner owns several different ores of different grades in same or different mines) the company has. It is further complicated by the complexities to extract and transport them. When the total of these costs is greater than its production price, the company will not be profitable. Understanding the market for ore futures is another discipline.

Many mining companies are in foreign countries such as Canada, Australia and countries in South America. Their financial statements of Canada and Australia are more trustworthy than those from most other emerging countries.

One potential problem of mining companies from many emerging countries is nationalization.

Mining rare earth ore is extremely risky when the profit depends on how China, a major producer of these ores, will price its ores. After China announced the export restrictions on rare earth elements, several non-Chinese companies announced to reopen their mines for rare earths but few make any profits as of 2013. Developed countries have stricter environmental regulations.

Coal suffers from the cleaner oil and gas.

Insurance companies

Insurance companies profit by:

1. The difference between the total premiums received and the total claims minus expenses in running the company.

2. How well they invest your premiums (you pay your premiums earlier than you may collect the claims).

They can protect the profits in #1 by restricting claims by natural disasters such as earthquakes and by re-insuring. However, a bad disaster could wipe out a lot of their profits.

Even if the insurance company shows you its investment portfolio, most of us, the retail investors, do not have the time and expertise to analyze it.

Emerging countries (not a sector)

Their financial statements especially from small companies cannot be trusted and many countries use different accounting standards. Emerging countries are where the economic growth is. I trade FXI, an ETF, rather than individual Chinese companies. I have lost a lot in small Chinese companies due to frauds. To check out whether the stock is an ADR, try ADR.COM.
https://www.adr.com/

Stocks with low volumes (not a sector)
Most likely you pay a high spread to trade these stocks. They can be manipulated easier. I remember I have a hard time to sell a

stock of this kind. The majority of this company is owned by one person.

For simplicity, I trade stocks with the average daily trade volume over 6,000 shares (double it if the price is $2 or less). The better way could be calculating the percent of your trade quantity / average daily trade volume to reduce the effect of penny stocks that have larger volumes due to the low prices. You need special skill to trade these stocks but it could be very profitable.

Good business and bad business

Banking is a good business. My deposit to them makes virtually zero interest, and they loan the same money making 3%. If they are more selective in loaning my money, they should make a good profit.

Restaurant is an easy business to open/run, but it is very hard to make good money. With the rising of minimal wages, it will get even tougher. That could be the reason of so many coupons today. The high-end restaurants are doing better due to the rising stock market. As of 8/2014, the new comers Noodles & Company (NDLS) and Potbelly (PBPB) are not doing well.

Airline is a tough business. You can tell by the average increase in fare in the last 10 years. It cannot even beat inflation. They have to charge you everything. The next frontier charge is the rest room (especially for long-distance flights). Now I understand why they call themselves "Frontier Air". As of 2014, it is quite profitable due to mergers and lower fuel cost.

There are several software companies that produce software such as the virus detecting programs and tax preparation software. The customers faithfully buy new versions every year. That's great business.

Retailing is a tough business. Look at the top 10 retailers 15 years ago, I can only find two including Macy's that are still surviving. Most are either bankrupted or being acquired. Even Macy's was at one time in financial trouble and was rescued by the late Run Run Shaw in Hong Kong.

(http://tonyp4idea.blogspot.com/2014/08/on-retail.html)

Related Filler

The retail industry is going thru the third wave if not already. The first one is Walmart and the second one is Amazon. After I visited one clothing store this Sunday, I realized a third wave is going on as Peter Lynch preached (i.e. learn from the mall).

The new retail store is formed by the exporter(s) in China who has strong ties to the manufacturers. They cut down the middle man (themselves). Judging from the customers hauling their over-loaded carts of merchandises with smiling faces, I know the wave has started if not already. There are several retail chains already all over the world even in small Ireland I visited recently. If you have stocks on low-end retail chains, watch out.

Afterthoughts

As of 8/2013, is emerging market oversold?
http://seekingalpha.com/article/1658252-have-emerging-markets-gotten-oversold

When an index of an emerging market is up by 10% and the currency exchange rate to USD is down by 20%, then it is not profitable.

Links

Nationalization: http://en.wikipedia.org/wiki/Nationalization
Spread: http://en.wikipedia.org/wiki/Bid-offer_spread
Insurance: http://seekingalpha.com/article/1239671-property-casualty-insurance-and-reinsurance-what-you-need-to-know

8   Technical analysis (TA)

Many times stock analysis based on fundamentals fails but technical analysis wins. Information such as a new product or a major lawsuit pending is not reflected timely in fundamentals but in technical analysis. It gives us guidance to the trend of a stock or the entire market.

The basics

Technical analysis (a.k.a. charting) is easier to learn than expected. It represents the trend of the market (a stock or a group of stocks) graphically. If more investors are in the market, a stock or a group of stocks, its trend is up until it changes. We divide the trends into short-term, intermediate-term and long-term.

The chartists usually do not consider fundamentals as they believe they have already been priced in the stock price and some fundamentals are not available to the public. To illustrate, a new drug has been discovered, the stock price of the company jumps initially by insiders and the informed. Its fundamental metrics do not show right away but many are buying to boost up the stock price.

The volume is a confirmation. When the stock moves up or down by 10% with a low volume, the trend is not confirmed.

The trend of the stock price is not straight line in most cases. Hence a trend line is usually drawn to indicate the direction of the stock. Many believe the stocks fluctuate in certain range (i.e. channels) and the chart draws the upper value (the resistance line) and the lower value (the support line).

When the price passes the channel, it is called a breakout. Darvas, one of the oldest and successful chartists, profited from the breakouts of the resistance line and believed the stock is close to the support line of the new channel. Hence it has a long way up.

If it is so simple, there will be no poor folks

It works most of the time, but do not bet all your money on it. For chartists, 51% is great (same for playing Black Jack). Some trends reverse very fast such as the bio drug stocks in 2015. You need to hedge your bets such as placing stop orders. Most do not want to spend their lives in watching the trend from a big screen. Most novices use too many technical indicators and lose to the professionals.

Simple Moving Average

The basic technical indicator is SMA-N. It is the average of the last N trade sessions. When N is 20 (or SMA-20), we classify it as short-term. Similarly, SMA-50 is intermediate-term and SMA-200 is long-term. I prefer 50, 100 and 250. This trend duration is important. For example, you do not want to place long-term bets using SMA-50 uptrend. There are many modifications to SMA that I do not find them better such as giving more weights to recent data. Finviz.com includes this information without charting.

Defining the trend periods is arbitrary. I use SMA-350 to detect market plunges and SMA-100 for stocks.

Trend is your best friend

Most use TA for trending for short durations. Investors can also use TA to time the entry and exit points for better potential profits. Value investors usually are patient and they do bottom fishing and they search for 'oversold' condition using RSI(14). Again high volume is a confirmation.

Many sites provide charting free of charge such as Yahoo!Finance. Finviz.com provides a lot of technical indicators without charting such as SMA% and RSI(14). It also provides screen searching for stocks that meet your technical analysis criteria.

TA patterns

There are many TA patterns such as Bollinger Bands and MACD. The patterns are based on the stock prices and many times they prove correct predictions especially on stocks with high volumes and high market caps.

Random remarks

Even if you do not use technical analysis, you should spend some time in learning it. It is better to marry fundamentals and TA. My random remarks are:

- The Institution investors (insurance companies, pension funds, mutual funds, etc.) use TA and they MOVE the market. A lot of times it becomes a self-fulfilling prophecy. It is better to join them as most of us cannot beat them.

- Day traders take advantage of the institution investors by spotting their trends.

- Most TA stocks should be good sizes and have large average daily volumes. I prefer to use TA on value stocks to prevent long-term loss.

- I do know some folks making big money using TA, but I know more making good money using fundamentals. Since TA predicts the market better in shorter term, its practitioners may have to pay higher taxes (in today's tax laws) in taxable accounts.

- Our objective should be making money at the least risk. Once you claim to belong to a certain group of either Fundamental or TA, you will be biased and forget your primary objective in investing.

Links
Fidelity video: Technical Analysis
https://www.fidelity.com/learning-center/technical-analysis/chart-types-video

Technical Analysis tutorial.
https://www.youtube.com/watch?v=GENBVwV8PMs
SMA tutorial.
https://www.youtube.com/watch?v=Na-ctpPsnks

9   An example on technical analysis

I have outlined how we can spot market plunge using TA and I use it to monitor the market every three months or so (recommend to do it every month and even more often when the market is risky). Here is an example on how to use it to trade individual stocks.

I have to admit I do not use TA that much on individual stocks and clearly I am not an expert in TA. If this article stirs up your interest, read more books or attend seminars / classes on TA. However, this book describes the basic and most useful technical indicators. There are many good and free articles from Investopedia on this topic. Personally I prefer to seek fundamentally sound companies at bargain prices and wait for their full appreciation. It has been proven to me.

TA is very useful for momentum and day traders. With the rising volumes, you can detect that the stocks are traded by managers of mutual funds, hedge funds, insurance companies and pension funds, and profit by riding on their wagons.

Some stocks are good for TA. Usually they are larger companies with above-average volumes and are fundamentally sound. Avoid the stocks that are trending downwards unless you're bottom fishing. Let me pick CSCO (a cyclical stock) for illustration. I bought it several times in 2012. I sold some in 2013 and 2014 making good profits. This is quite different from what short-term traders would use the following information for.

The green line is 50-day simple moving average (SMA) for the following chart using one year data.

If it does not display clearly on a small screen, type the following on the browser on your PC.

http://ebmyth.blogspot.com/2013/05/chart-for-ta-example.html

Buy the stock when it is above its SMA and sell when it is below. Following the chart would make good money based on this simple rule. Also, practice the strategy "Sell on May 1, Buy back on Nov. 1".

Not all stocks follow this profitable pattern. Fundamentalists may try to pick the bottom in late July while chartists enter positions on its upward trend. The chartists have an advantage to stay away from stocks in their downward trend.

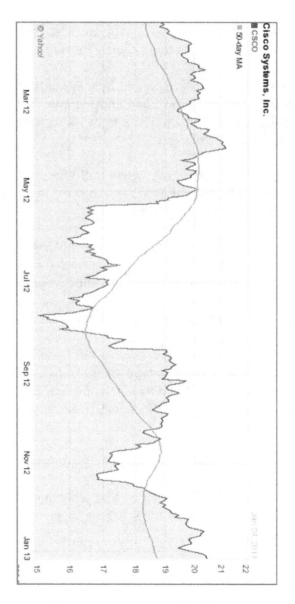

Table: CSCO 50-day SMA   Source: Yahoo!Finance

We can improve the trades by:

- Use different moving average in number of days (50 in this example) and other indicators such as EMA (a moving average that weighs higher on more recent data). It may improve prediction accuracy and/or cut down the number of trades. RSI(14) suggests overbought / oversold conditions.

- Instead of selling the stock for cash, consider selling the stock short. Selling short is not for beginners for sure.

- The accuracy is usually improved by a separate chart for the sector the stock belongs to and another one for the market. For CSCO, you can use an ETF for network companies and SPY (or a similar ETF) to represent the market.

  In theory and in theory only, when both the stock, the sector that the stock is in and the market all move down, it has a high chance to move down, and vice versa.

  We use 50 days (in SMA) for short-term holding of stocks (90 days for longer holding), 90 days for the sector ETF and 350 days for SPY. Again, 'days' is actually 'trade sessions'.

TA is not for most fundamentalists but it should be used

For a bargain hunter like me, TA would not benefit me a lot for picking stocks at the bottoms. I would try to pick up CSCO with prices ranging from 15-17 and all below the moving average line that TA would not show me a Buy signal. However, for short-term swing traders TA is a Godsend.

To me, TA is good indicator for growth and momentum for short-term trading. Some fundamentalists may use TA for entry and exit point. Some recommend buying the stock when the price is above the SMA-200 (same as SMA-200% is positive that can be readily obtained from finviz.com).

It is profitable for 'Buy High and Sell Higher' if you can protect your profits effectively. This is also called 'Buy at a reasonable cost'. One's opinion.

In selecting a tool, you have to understand how, why to use it and whether it fits your investing style. I use TA for market timing for the entire market more than on individual stocks. When I have more time, I would use TA more frequently. My portfolio has too many stocks that I should cut down.

Most of us cannot spot the bottom of a stock; I had some successes but most likely they were due to luck. When a stock is moving up from the bottom, there is a good chance it will move further up. TA shows it and its volume confirms it.

Conclusion
Even a fundamentalist like me can benefit a lot by using TA. This book touches the very basics of TA but the most useful TA indicators.

Besides monitoring the fundamentals of the stocks you bought once every 6 months, you should analyze their technical more often (1 month to 3 months depending on your available time). When the market is risky (close to the SMA average), run the SMA chart more frequently (say once a week).

A joke, a nightmare or reality

I got a call from Buffett asking me to lead their stock research. I asked him why for a nobody; you may be asking the same question. No kidding.

He told me that he should have read my book Scoring Stocks to buy Apple instead of IBM in May, 2013. It would save his company millions of dollars minus $10 for my book. Not to mention the market timing technique that had worked in the last two major market plunges.

I told him, "OK, I'll beat your mediocre returns of the last 5 years."

I told him, "I cannot beat the market as you are the market especially after your expensive fees. In addition, I do not know how to avoid day traders from riding my wagon in trading. Also most of my big profits were made in small stocks that your fund cannot trade besides owning the company." I woke up trembling. I'm glad it is only a nightmare

10   Bollinger Bands & MACD

Bollinger Bands has been proven useful for traders. In theory, the stock is traded between the upper band and the lower band forming an envelope. For more info, click the following link.

http://www.investopedia.com/terms/b/bollingerbands.asp

The following chart was drawn by Yahoo!Finance for CSCO from 8/7/2012 to 8/7/2014 (today) selecting Bollinger Bands for the 50 days as a parameter. If you trade more often, use 20 days. If the chart is too small to display on your screen, enter the following in your PC's browser.
http://ebmyth.blogspot.com/2014/08/screen-csco-bollinger-bands-50.html

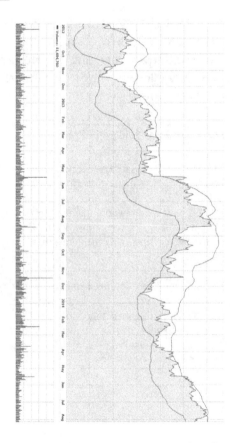

Bollinger Bands 50 Days.   Source: Yahoo!Finance

You buy the stock when the price is close to the lower band and sell the stock when it is close to the upper band.

When the stock price passes the upper band, it is called a breakout. Similar for the stock falling below the lower band.

From the above, we should make some good money but lose some opportunities as it did break out.

It is advisable to use at least one more technical indicator. I recommend RSI(14), which is also accessible from Yahoo!Finance or similar sites. When it is above 70, it is overbought, so I recommend selling the stock. When it is below 30, it is oversold, so I recommend buying the stock.

MACD

MACD, Moving Average Convergence Divergence, is an effective momentum (i.e. short-term) indicator used by most traders. When the stock price is crossing above the zero line, it is a buy and vice versa. Again, try to master SMA and RSI(14) first. Using too many indicators usually harm you more than help you.

A joke

I got an email from my potential congressman as follows:
The Supreme Court has ruled that there cannot be a Nativity Scene in the United States' Capital this Christmas Season. This isn't for any religious reason. They simply have not been able to find Three Wise Men in the Nation's Capital. The Search for a Virgin continues. There was no problem, however, finding enough asses to fill the stable.

My reply:
Beg to differ. All congressmen including yourself are wise men if you compare your bank account before your term and after. You can find a lot of virgins but you've to lower your age requirement or change the definition of a virgin. For definition, borrow the example from Clinton's no smoker policy: As long as you do not exhale, you're a non-smoker. Change the word 'exhale' with many words I can think of but they are not too polite to write them down here - just in case the naive Sister Teresa is reading my blog secretly. It appears to be a fact that there are more mouths kissing asses than asses available to be kissed. Hence, we really have a shortage of asses.

11   TA for Sector Rotation, Reentry & Peak

There are 3 uses of TA for sector rotation.

1. Detect sector plunge and when to reenter the market after plunges.
2. Regular use (usually after its recovery from a plunge).
3. Detect market plunges and/or sector plunges.

#3 has been described on the chapter Spotting Market Plunges and it will not be repeated here.

The difference in #1 and #2 is in the number of days in SMA (Single Moving Average). Use 350 for sector plunge and reentry.

Use 30, 60, 90 or 120 for regular use (i.e. after the reentry from a market plunge) depending on how frequently you rotate. If you rotate in 60 days, use 60 for the average of number of days.

Exit / Reenter a sector ETF

To illustrate, the following example uses XHB (an ETF for the housing sector). Use the same chart for other sector ETFs such as VGK for Europe.

Produce the following chart by using Yahoo!Finance. Enter XHB and select Interactive Chart. Select SMA and then 350 days. Select Max for 'From'.

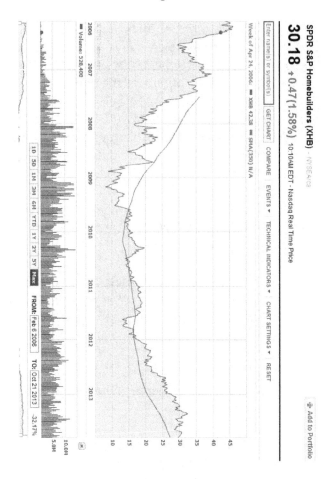

Source: Yahoo!Finance. XHB on 350 SMA.

- Exit when the price falls below the red, single-moving average (the SMA) and enter when it is over the SMA. All the dates and prices are approximate and for illustration only.

- I use Max for the period. Let's assume the chart instructed us to exit at $45 around 2006 and reenter on August, 2009 missing a loss of about $30 per share. Not too bad!

- There are brief exits and reentries before 2012. I call it noises. The gains and losses are negligible. However, make sure you exit and also reenter. If you use 60 days instead of 350 days in this example, you have more noises. If you trade the ETF more often, then you use 60 or 90 days. It depends on your risk tolerance and your time to trade. Sometimes the performance makes a difference in selecting shorter days, but not all the time.

- From the end of 2012 to today (10-2013), it gains more than 40% compared to -32% for the period for buy-and-hold. A difference of 62%! Even a difference of 10% would be great.

- The chart works at least for this period. It is every one's guess whether it will still work in the future. I bet it will but as in life nothing is guaranteed.

- When a housing stock, the housing sector (XHB) and the general stock market all above their respective SMAs, the stock most likely will appreciate (again nothing is guaranteed).

- From my other chapters, the offending sector (housing and finance for 2007 market plunge) takes about two years to recover from the bottom.

  I interpreted the bottom was 10-2007, so the recovery would start in 10-2009. If you bought XHB in 10-2009, you would have gained about 100% today (10-22-2013).

- Some sectors never recover such as the internet and some high tech companies in 2000.

Now, it is your turn to try out the chart. This time, use 60 for the number of days in SMA.

Afterthoughts

- We have discussed how to use TA to spot market crashes and individual stocks. TA can help us to determine a sector. For my purpose, I usually use 90-day moving average on an ETF for that industry, but 350-day moving average for detecting sector plunges / reentries.

- The big boys (hedge fund managers) moved their money into GOOG and AMZN solely to make a ton of cash when AAPL reached $700 and they will move their investment out of AMZN (too high value as of 1-2013) or GOOG back into AAPL.

  Instead of fighting the big movers, join them by using the tool of TA. Make good money by winning the second place of a horse race.

- A stock will always go up and down for more than several days in a row. Take advantage of the trend and make some quick money if you are a short-term trader.

- If all the following are above the single moving average (SMA) line, most likely (most and not all) the stock price will rise in next month:

  1. 350-day SMA of SPY (representing the market).
  2. 60-day (or 90-day) SMA of the sector ETF that represents the sector the stock is in.
  3. 30-day SMA (or 20 for some folks) of the stock and it passes our (or your) scoring system.

  Most technicians use 20, 50 and 200 days for moving averages for stocks. To save you time, use finviz.com to obtain the % of the stock deviates from its moving averages. When it is positive, it is usually a buy.

- Norman:
  With cyclical dividend paying stocks, entry and exit points can be equivalent to yield. For example buy CAT at 3% yield and sell it at 1% yield.

- A book mentioned to me on TA: Stan Weinstein's book, "Secrets for Profiting in Bull & Bear Markets".

- If you are a customer of Fidelity, try the option to include all indicators in charting a stock. To illustrate of using index S&P500, use .SPX (^GSPC in Yahoo!Finance).

- Sectors can also be divided by market cap. Use the same charts to find the trend of small cap for example.

- When TA tells you to sell a stock, try to find the reasons by using google, SeekingAlpha, Yahoo!Finance board, calling the company, etc.

- More related articles.

Based on performance.
http://stockcharts.com/help/doku.php?id=chart_school:trading_strategies:sector_rotation_roc

Fidelity.
https://www.fidelity.com/learning-center/trading-investing/markets-sectors/sector-rotation-introduction

A subscription service.
http://www.sectortimingreport.com/articles/sector-rotation.html

---

Tip

As of 3/2014, TSLA, AMAZ, NFLX are all over-priced by most fundamental metrics. However, they are the darlings of institution investors. My advice is not to short them as you cannot fight the city hall. If you're the lucky owners, use trailing stops to protect your profit. They will plunge when they are no longer the darlings of the institution investors – they do rotate as they did to Apple.

IV Strategy 4: Sectors in market cycle

Here are the favorable sectors in different phases of a market cycle. Here is my suggestion

Market Phase	Favorable		Unfavorable
Early Recovery	Financial, Technology, Industrial		Energy, Telecom, Utilities
Up	Technology, Industrial, Housing		
Peak	Mineral, Health Care, Energy, Long-Term Bond, Consumer Discretionary		
Bottom	Consumer Staples, Utilities		Consumer Discretionary, Technology, Industrial, Long-Term & high yield Bond

The sectors that cause the recession usually take longer time to recover. In 2000, the technology sector was not favorable in the Early Recovery phase, contrary to the above table. In 2007, the financial sector was not favorable in the Early Recovery phase. These are the "offending" sectors that cause the plunges.

In a recession, we usually cannot cut down on consumer staples and utilities, but we can cut down buying consumer gadgets. Companies usually postpone investing in equipment and systems during a recession and expand when the economy is humming.

All the description in Section I and III apply here. The next chapter describes the market cycle and how I define he phases of a market cycle.

Sectors according to the business cycle

Market Cycle is usually ahead of the Business (economic) cycle by 6 months as a rough prediction. In the 2008 market cycle, it is not due to the excessive printing of money.

During a recession some sectors such as Consumer Staples and Health Care work better than other sectors such as Technology. They will be opposite from above during the go-go era when consumers have more money to buy non-essential goods and companies have money to invest.

Some sectors are more volatile than others. Some sectors such as Health Care would be benefited by the growing or aging global population.

Sectors	Major Industries	Favorable
Basic Materials	Metals, Mining, Chemicals	High inflation / Growing economy
Consumer Discretionary	Auto, Building, High-end Retail	Low interest rate
Consumer Staples	Food	Recession
Energy	Oil, Gas, Exploration	Growing economy
Industrial	Machines	Economic recovery
Health Care	Delivery, Drugs, Biotech	Recession for Delivery
Financial	Bank, Insurance	High interest, Growing economy
Technology	Computer, software	Growing economy
Utilities	Electricity, Gas	Recession

12   Market cycle

"Bull markets are born on pessimism, grow on skepticism, mature on optimism, and die on euphoria" - Sir John Templeton

The stock market has cycles as our practical interpretation of the above. It is about five years apart, but it fluctuates widely. I divide it into four stages: Bottom, Early Recovery, Up and Peak.

My defined four stages of a market cycle

We need to apply the right investing strategies to each of the four stages of the cycle.

- **Bottom**

  I would not invest for at least the first six months (or even a year) after the big plunge starts, which could lose over 25% in a few months. The exceptions are investing in contra ETFs and selling short for aggressive investors.

  I estimate it will take a year from the start of the plunge to the bottom, so I will normally sell stocks early in the plunge and do not buy stocks that are in the sector (sometimes sectors) that causes the bubble for about two years after the plunge. Do not buy the stocks even they do not have a chance to recover.

  At the bottom, the high-yield corporate bonds (i.e. junk bonds) would prosper when the interest rate is decreasing to simulate the economy.

  From mid-2007 to mid-2008, bonds suffered as the investors thought the sky was falling down - it was to those who lost the jobs and/or their houses. After that, some bonds especially the long-term bonds appreciated about 50% for the following year.

  The government lowered the interest rate and these bond prices with high interest rate surged. Correct timing in buying bonds could be very profitable.

Long-term bonds have more impact by the interest rate: The lower the interest rate, the higher the bond prices of higher-yield bonds. The older bonds with higher interest rates are more valuable to the newer bonds with lower interest rates.

I define this period of the bottom from the start of the plunge to the start of Early Recovery.

- **Early Recovery**

It usually starts after one year from the plunge; no one can pin point the exact time consistently. By this time preferably earlier, we should have closed out all positions in contra ETFs and shorts.

Roughly speaking, October, 2007 (some use 2008) is the start of the market plunge. March, 2009 is the end of the bottom stage and the start of the early recovery stage of the 2007 cycle. However, every market cycle is different in where it starts and ends.

The one-year gain from the bottom is most profitable. It usually gains over 25% in a year from the market bottom. I, a conservative investor, had huge gain using some leverage in my largest taxable account in 2009. I recalled I had a similar return in 2003 from my memory.

In this phase, value is a better parameter than growth in searching stocks. If your investment subscription provides a composite value score and a composite timing score, the sort parameter of your screened stocks could be "Composite Value / Composite Timing" in descending order. Select the top stocks in this order. Still have to analyze the top-screened stocks.

Expected P/E is a good metric. However, most companies may be losing money at this stage. Those companies that can last for more than one year with its cash reserve are potential good buys. The best appreciated stocks are beaten companies that have precious technologies and good customer bases. They could be candidates to be acquired if they are small enough.

- **Up**

  Usually the growth metrics such as PEG could be better than the value metrics such as expected P/E during this phase. Most stocks are winners except contra ETFs and shorting stocks. When the growth stocks are making headlines and the defensive stocks are being dumped, this is the hint that we're well into the Up phase of the market cycle.

  Locate stocks with growth metrics such as favorable PEG and high SMA-200% (from Finviz.com). Do not be scared on how much they have already appreciated. The strategy "Buy High and Sell Higher" works in this phase. Protect your profits with stops.

  Ensure they have value too. Skip the stocks with expected P/Es higher than 35 unless there are good reasons. Most stocks will gain due to the tide of the market. However, when they're overbought (RSI(14) over 60), be careful. When institutional investors sell these stocks, they will crash.

- **Peak**

  When everyone makes easy money and the interest rate is high, watch out. Stop loss and/or stop limit should be used to protect your investment. Check out whether there is any bubble that would be burst like the internet in 2000 and the finance (and housing) in 2007.

  Internet crisis is easy to spot, but not the financial crisis. In 2007 we had a cycle longer than the average which is about 5 years. The plunge is very fast and very steep – thanks to the institution investors who drive the market down.

  Run the technical analysis chart described in the Chapter on Spotting Big Market Plunges at least monthly (weekly if you have time). Protect your investment. Do not fall in love with any stock (you can buy it back later at a deep discount). Making the last buck is a fool's game.

Accumulate cash according to your risk tolerance. A retiree or a conservative investor would accumulate from 25% to 50% and should be ready to move to all cash when the plunge starts.

We can lower the cash percent if we use enough stop loss protection. Be psychologically prepared that the stock market may still rise for a while. There is no perfect market timing.

The 2007 Cycle

The market plunged starting in 10-2007 and ending in 3-2009 (bottom), started to recover in 3-2009 (early recover), and trended up from 2010 to 1-2013 (the up phase of the market cycle). As of 3/2016, it is the peak phase defined by me.

As of 1/2013, we have recovered all the market losses since 2007. However, as of 7/2014, the economy has not fully recovered compared to the economy before the plunge. The employment judging by the medium salary has not fully recovered and the economy is not expanding. It is uncommon that the economy does not follow the market. It is due to the excessive supply of money by the government and partly due to globalization to allow companies hire overseas.

Although a W-shaped recession seldom happens, we have a chance today. We hope we do not have a depression and/or the similar lost decades that Japan has been experiencing. Some may conclude we are close to complete a market cycle from 2007 to 2016. As of 2016, the economy is recovering slowly and we're better than most other global economies.

Again, market timing is not an exact science as it involves irrational human beings and government interventions. The timing using market cycle described here is a guideline as it is hard to time it exactly.

The average market cycle is about 5 years, but they fluctuate. If we consider 2007 as the plunge, we have about 8 years of this cycle as of 2015.

In a typical cycle (few are typical), we have about one year in each of the 4 phases I defined (plunge, early recovery, up and peak).

Events/Triggers

There are financial events and triggers that cause the transition of one phase of the market cycle to another. They usually do not change the sequence of the phases (say not from Peak to Early Recovery), but they may change the duration of the phase. Examples are:

* The government announcing change of the interest rate,
* Change of employment, and
* Change of GNP.

Sectors in a market cycle (my suggestion)

Market Phase	Favorable		Unfavorable
Early Recovery	Financial, Technology, Industrial		Energy, Telecom, Utilities
Up	Technology, Industrial, Housing		
Peak	Mineral, Health Care, Energy, Long-Term Bond, Consumer Discretionary		
Bottom	Consumer Staples, Utilities		Consumer Discretionary, Technology, Industrial, Long-Term & high-yield Bond

The sectors that cause the recession usually take longer time to recover. In 2000, the technology sector was not favorable in the Early Recovery phase, contrary to the above table. In 2007, the financial sector was not favorable in the Early Recovery phase. These are the "offending" sectors that cause the plunges.

In a recession, we usually cannot cut down on consumer staples and utilities, but we can cut down buying consumer gadgets. Companies usually postpone investing in equipment and systems during a recession and expand when the economy is humming. The government usually lowers the interest rate right after the plunge to stimulate the economy.

Conclusion

When the market is about to plunge or change from one stage to another, run the described chart more frequently and read more articles written by the experts. In 2000, one article described that it could fit all the employees of a specific high-tech company into a conference room of any major corporation and the two companies had similar market cap. This article drove me to unload all of my stocks in high tech.

Again, market timing is not an exact science but it is based on educated guesses. The better guesses should have more rights than wrongs in the long term. Our actions depend on our risk tolerance. Be careful on using any new strategy that has not been fully understood and proven. Since 2000, market timing is very important to your financial health with two market plunges with an average of about 45% loss.

Afterthoughts

- The Dow Theory has a lot of followers in detecting market directions. In a nutshell, the market heading upwards is confirmed by the Industrial Index and the Transportation Index (less important in today's market especially with internet sales such as songs and movies), and vice versa. As of 4/2014, the two indexes are not in uniform.
  http://finance.yahoo.com/blogs/talking-numbers/this-is-a-130-year-old-warning-sign-for-stocks-231901097.html

  - The bear market has the following three phases.

    1. The market is over-valued.
    2. Corporations are not doing well with decreasing earnings and sales.
    3. Investors are selling due to fears.

    It is the reverse for a bull market: 1.The market is under-valued. 2. The market increases due to increasing corporate profits/sales and 3. Investors are buying due to greed.

- Investopedia has several articles on this topic.
  http://www.investopedia.com/terms/b/businesscycle.asp

- The yield curve could predict the interest rate change and hence the economy. There are three main types of yield curve shapes: normal, flat and inverted.

  A normal yield curve is one in which longer maturity bonds have a higher yield. It is similar that the long-term CD should have a higher interest rate than the short-term CD.

  When the shorter-term yields are higher than the longer-term yields, it indicates an upcoming recession. A flat yield curve indicates the economy is transiting. Now, you've read the essence of a book on this topic costing about $50 to buy.

  However especially today, it does not mean anything as the government supplies too much money to stimulate the economy unsuccessfully. My simple chart described using SMA-350 (Simple Moving Average for 350 trade sessions) which depends on the stock price works better. Click here for The dynamic yield curve.

  The interest rate plays a role too. The easy money encourages folks to borrow money to buy stocks and companies to acquire other companies.

- Total Market Cap / GNP ratio is hotly debated on the market value. Different from the traditional 100%, I would suggest that the boundary ratio should be 130%. If it is over 130%, the market is over-valued and vice versa.
  http://www.investopedia.com/terms/m/marketcapgdp.asp

13   Actions for different stages of a market cycle

There are different strategies for the different stages of the market cycle.

Strategies during market plunges

The market plunge is defined as the period between the market peak and the market bottom. It usually lasts for one year or two.

When you spot the potential plunge, consider the following actions. It depends on your risk tolerance and your investment style.

1. Contrary to popular belief, parking cash is a strategy too. Cash is needed later to move back to equities.

2. Be conservative: Buy stocks based on value and not based on momentum. Reduce your new purchases and take profits especially on momentum stocks. I buy one stock for every two or three stocks I sold during this stage.

3. Protect your portfolio with stop orders. It is one of the few times I recommend stop orders. If you watch the market every day, just place market orders when your stock falls to a specific price.

4. Buy contra ETFs for aggressive investors.

5. Sell cover calls. I prefer to sell the stocks I own.

6. Older folks may not want to sell the stocks with huge gains (due to tax consideration) or stocks that give them income stream of dividends. They can use options to protect potential losses for the stocks they own.

What to do after the plunge

In the first year after the start of the plunge, do not start to buy unless they are very good values. Aggressive investors should start closing their short positions/put options and selling contra ETFs.

When the market plunges, it usually takes at least one year to recover as investors believe they have to sell to protect their remaining nest eggs. Those sectors that cause the bubble will take even longer to recover.

After the plunge, watch out for the interest rate. If it is still high, it is the best time to buy high-yield bonds (i.e. junk bonds). Ensure that the corporation issuing the bonds would not bankrupt; the bonds from the old GM in 2007 lost most of their values. They will appreciate when the interest rate drops that the government would routinely do to stimulate the economy. 2008 is not a good year to invest in stocks and bonds except the contra ETFs and selling shorts, but 2009 definitely is (it is my Early Recovery phase of the market cycle).

Personally I prefer not to buy any stocks until the chart tells us to reenter the market. It is the fear that investors do not want to reenter the market. The market will always recover as in the past history.

Even before the recovery, some sectors (called consumer staple) are doing better such as health care, foodstuffs, utilities and pharmaceuticals that are always in demand. Interest-sensitive sectors such as housing and auto will suffer disproportionately. They are also called cyclical stocks. Consumer Discretionary are sectors that suffer a lot in a recession such as high tech products.

What to do in early recovery and after

When the market is starting to recovery (2003 and 2009 in the last two market cycles), the potential profit is the highest. Buy deeply-valued stocks on companies that have been beaten. They will recover with the highest appreciation potential. I call it the bottom fishing strategy.

Larger companies are fishing too to acquire smaller companies that fit into their corporate synergy or small companies with the technology and/or the customer base they need.

Valued stocks could be defined a little differently in this phase. Many times P/E is not a good metric as most companies are losing money. 2003 is such a year. If you expect the recession will end in 2 years and the company has enough cash to survive in two years based on its annual burn rate, then it would be a buy candidate.

In both 2003 and 2009, I spotted at least one company that was acquired by larger company. From my memory, one company in 2003 was acquired by IBM giving me more than 2 times return. In 2009, at least three companies were acquired giving me an average annualized return of over 200%.

Momentum strategy rewards us best from the end of the early recovery phase to the peak phase. The up phase started in 2004 for 2000 market cycle and 2010 in the 2007 market cycle.

Note. The parameters of SMA-200, SMA-350, SMA-90, etc. and RSI are different for market exit/reentry, correction exit and individual stocks. They're the guidelines only. Stocks are more volatile than the market and are very different among them. Hence, define the 'days' according to the historical pattern of the individual stock and how often you trade them.

V   Strategy 5: Country sectors

The current events as of 5/2014, Russia (Ukraine incident) and S.E. Asia (the Vietnam riots) are not good countries to invest at least for the next two or three years. However, Vietnam with low wages could be the next China. As of 2016, the US is still a good place to invest. Again Section I and Section III apply here also. For example, use the P/E to evaluate an ETF corresponding to this country.

14   My Coconut Theory

Coconut Theory

In a tropical island, every one sleeps under a coconut tree assigned to him. He wakes up only when a coconut falls on his head once in a while; he does not have to think when he just wakes up and eats. He eats the coconut and goes back to sleep. He is lazy due to the nice weather (no need to find shelter) and the nice resource (the coconut tree). He is happy and rich by his own standard. However, he is lazy, fat, and stupid due to the lack of any need to work, exercise, and think out of his 'perfect' environment.

The worst that happens to the natives is borrowing coconuts from other natives with the coconut tree as collateral or cut down the coconut tree to make a canoe without plans on how to replenish coconuts in the future.

This is a simple theory. It can be used to explain how and why many countries are rich, poor, and continue to be so. Let's check how this theory stacks up with countries.

U.S.A.

The U.S. is the richest country due to its developed and highly educated citizens, hard-working immigrants and the huge natural resources per capita (i.e. having a lot of coconuts in my theory). The U.S. is declining as we spend more time enjoying our wealth (borrowing coconuts so he can eat more; on credit – living beyond our means!) rather than creating more wealth (i.e. eating up most of the coconuts and not planting new coconut trees in my theory).

The wealth is equivalent to the bountiful of coconut trees that were available originally and the many that were planted by our ancestors. There were fewer natives to consume the total number of coconuts, so there was a surplus of coconuts grown, eventually to be given away (as welfare and entitlements).

Because of WW2, most coconut trees in the world were destroyed while ours were fine. We were rich to ship our better coconuts to the rest of the world.

God gave us plenty of natural resources, good soil and climatic wealth (coconuts hidden under the land) and hopefully we continue to be wealthy. Unfortunately, we're now consumers (of coconuts) instead of producers (planting new coconut trees).

Norway

Norway is the richest to its population group (3 millions) while Brunei is richest in its own category. Norway has more money than God because of its long coastal line and its intelligently governed oil wealth, so everything works better there. I hate to compare any country to Norway as most likely we are comparing Apples to Melons.

From its long coast line Norway has rich off-shore oil fields and abundant fish exports which is second in the world-- only 6% of its export, after China but far, far #1 per capita wise. Because of the world's oil addition and food dependence secures its income flow.

Peru has a long coast line, but it is not wealthy. My theory does not apply fully here, as there are always exceptions. It could be Norway's educated citizens, close location to its trade partners and buying assets around the world (planting more coconut trees). The dividend payments allow Norway to prosper for decades. They have about 600 billion sovereign fund to be shared by 3 million citizens. Simple math!

Iceland

Some smart guys suggested cutting down all the coconut trees to make canoes so they can earn a rich life by fishing. The world loans them with coconuts. When the fishing fails, their land is lost with no coconuts and no coconut trees left. Do not bet all the coconuts in one venture.

Singapore and SE Asia

Singapore is rich due to its important location for the sea route for trade and commerce, as well as being the cultural intersection between the east and the west and its industrious citizens (most are Chinese). When the hard-working folks land on a land of coconuts (i.e. resources), they naturally become rich.

Mekong River is a good resource providing fishing, irrigation, transportation, and fertile land in the delta for SE Asia. Hence, SE Asia should be rich, and at the same time attracts hard-working immigrants from India and China to enhance their wealth.

Japan

Japan has few natural resources. Its only resource is the educated and hard-working citizens. With a decreasing population and the policy not welcoming immigrants, Japan will face problems.

Haiti

Haiti used to have enough coconuts for its small population. French imported African slaves to the sugar cane plantation and changed the allocation of natural resources per capita. Coupled with frequent natural disasters and bad governance, Haiti becomes the poorest country in the world. Corruption in poor countries is natural.

UAE

When the west helped UAE to explore its oil resources (the hidden coconuts under the sand) about 50 years ago, UAE becomes the richest country on earth. She expands in different areas and it could be over-expanded. When the oil dries up in 100 or so years and/or the shale energy competes better, they could be in big trouble.

Russia

Russia is a country full of resources (coconuts). Its citizens become lazy having a good time under the 'coconut' tree. Chinese are just the opposite. That's why the Russians hire the hard-working Chinese to tender farm in the border while they enjoy life with plenty of Vodka ☺.

The primary reason why USSR fell was the temporary low prices of their resources oil and timber (coconuts). Trying to be #1 was another reason.

China

China has roughly 20% of the world population, but it has far less than 20% of the world resources (coconuts). For example, it has only 6% of the world land area. The situation was worsened in the last 250 years during the Opium Wars, and then semi colonization by the eight countries (helping the opium pushers). It bankrupted China by their colonial masters. It caused massive migration to escape from the land without coconuts. It was followed by WW2, war lord era and then the bad governance. Their bitter lessons ensure this generation and the next generation to work hard and be smart. When they do not have 'coconut trees' (the colonial masters cut most of them down), you have to work hard or die.

China ranks #2 in the economy. It is only important to its trading partners. Its own citizens care about their living standard which is about the middle in the rank of all countries.

Ancient civilizations too

Greece, Iran, India, China and Italy are among the oldest civilizations. Most do not do well in today's economy and many of their citizens have immigrated to other countries. My theory suggests that they have exhausted their coconuts (farm land and metals) throughout the long history. Hence, they have to migrate to lands with more coconuts.

To illustrate, there is a huge discrepancy in natural resources (oil, metal and farm land) between China and the U.S., which has a relatively short history.

Corporations too

Microsoft was a tougher company with more innovations fifteen years ago than today. However, they are enjoying easy profitability of upgrades of Windows and Office (coconuts planted by their ancestors). For a long time, she only has one successful new product, the Xbox. Her managers are counting their bonuses instead of taking risk. The Coconut Theory works again.

Rich families too

It is very rare to have rich families that last over three generations. The first generation grows the wealth (planting coconuts), the second generation enjoys the wealth, and the third or fourth generation usually becomes poor due to the easy life.

Conclusion

So far, no one tells me that this theory has been 'discovered' by others. Shamelessly I claim it is mine. To me, it is just common sense.

Afterthoughts

- I did not have a coconut tree (i.e. financial aid or money from my dad), and that is why I worked two jobs in my first summer while attending college here. The first one was a bus boy job from 5 pm to 10 pm. The other one was cleaning slot machines from 4 am to noon for 5 and most likely 7 days a week. Lack of coconut makes you desire to work hard or you die. With an average IQ, I can make it by working hard in a land of coconuts.

  My children have too many coconuts and they live in a more lavish life style than the old man. They ask me why I work that hard during my retirement or why I still go to Burger King with a coupon even they do not treat me like a king.

- Using Norman's opinion, the problem with a small place filled with coconuts is someone would likely to colonize you and steal your coconuts as happened to Norway during WWII. Similar to China about 250 years ago. Once a while, need to cut down one among many coconut trees to make spears to protect the rest of the coconuts.

On China.

Music.
https://www.youtube.com/watch?v=2yvaPDaE95g&list=PLB2CFDC94ED219184

Why China is rising.
http://tonyp4idea.blogspot.com/2014/08/why-china-is-rising.html

Uncle Deng.
http://tonyp4idea.blogspot.com/2014/08/uncle-deng.html

Pictures.
http://www.bing.com/images/search?q=chinese+photographs&qpvt=chinese+photographs&FORM=IGRE

Amazing circus and ballet
https://www.youtube.com/watch?v=aQmYBJwZGZE

---

15   Aging global population

The aging of the global population is due to the proliferation of baby boomers after WW2.

- India will suffer from the population explosion despite the abundance of younger citizens.

  They will eat up all the limited food and consume most of its limited natural resources. They will run out of water in 100 years which is also controlled by China as more water will be directed to the north of Tibet. There are too many problems that cannot be resolved easily. There is no bright future for India. I wish I were wrong as a poor India would affect the rest of the world.

  http://en.wikipedia.org/wiki/South-North_Water_Diversion_Project

  They classify themselves literate if they can write their name in any language compared to 1,500 Chinese characters for China. Chinese have nine years of compulsory education. These statistics are just being manipulated.

  Source: Ted Talk.
  http://www.ted.com/talks/yasheng_huang.html

  The brain drain is alarming as the most privileged / educated do not want to wait for India's infrastructure, its economy and its governance to be fixed.

  I hope rich countries like the U.S. will not take too many doctors / nurses from poor countries such as India as we're doing now. This is the worst disservice to a poor country. We deprive thousands from medical care for each doctor we import. Why do we send our doctors to help the poor while we take their doctors? It just does not make sense. There should be more foreign aid allocated to medical training to poor countries.

Just compare the sub way system and the number of high-rises in India to any Tier 3 city in China. The top Indian city just built its sub way recently in 2011 while Hong Kong has developed into a modern metropolitan with a modern and extensive sub way system many years ago. As of 2012, more than half of India's population lives in less than $2.50 a day (the UN definition of poverty is $2.50 / day).

India has to understand its problems first before they can fix them. It has to fight inefficiency, corruption (partly due to inefficiency) and protectionism (to improve quality and encourage foreign investment). Copying China's model is a good idea. China's model is to create specific economic zones close to a port with the essential infrastructure for that area. You need to build infrastructure like highway, electricity... for that area first. It should target its products first to the foreign market and then include the home market.

The 2011 Indian Kolkata airport has limited road access while the 1980 Hong Kong airport is supported by extensive suspension bridges. Without the road access support, any airport would not be world-class as demonstrated by all major airports in the world. Documentaries on both projects are available from Netflix.

Some told me it could be old, wealthy families controls India's economy and they do not want changes. I argue the opposite is true. Expensive projects usually allow the corrupt rich and the local governments to steal money from public projects.

- China still has plenty of cheap labor.
  Cheap labor will be minor but education will be important as they need to move up to the next level of industrialization with higher-value products. China is already there in many areas.

China has its own problems, and plenty of them, but demographics are not the major one. Gender imbalance, pollution and corruption are many among others.

Click this link http://bit.ly/ybAnoW to compare India and China.

- Russia and Brazil still thrive on commodities and oil as long as global economy grows.

  Russians fit my Coconut Theory. They become lazier (and more intoxicated with Vodka ☺) as the economy continually grows from its wealth of natural resources including oil. As long as the global economy is humming, there are demands for these resources, and vice versa.

- Africa and some S. American countries.

  The explosive population will bring miseries to their worlds. There will be more wars for food and life expectancies are already lowered. The citizens will migrate legally and illegally to richer countries like the U.S. for a better living. If the farming technology to produce more food with less farm land did not improve drastically over the last 50 years, the world's supply of food now would not meet the demand. As 2012 closes, there are higher food prices due to the floods and droughts all over the world. It will continually be rougher for the poor countries that cannot afford to pay for it especially when China and India have more cash from their exports.

- The U.S.

  In 2023, the U.S. may look like Japan is today as most developed countries whose populations shrunk to below zero growth. However, the U.S.'s black and Hispanics have a higher fertility rate and the U.S. has more immigrants than all other countries combined. The U.S. will have its different problems / advantages as below.

  The U.S. welcomes immigrants (as opposed to Japan). Most qualified Indians are welcome and so are Chinese (who come for economic reasons, to escape from pollution, or because of corruption prosecutions).

  In the U.S., today's minorities will become the majority. If you look at their high school dropout rate, social welfare recipient percent, prisoner percent, etc., we do not have a bright future. There will be more political leaders from these groups as we usually vote for politicians that belong to the same race as ours. These are facts and it might be offensive to you if you're a minority.

When we do not have jobs for everyone, a large population is a big burden. We have recent college graduates begging for any job for years, lines for unemployment and welfare offices are getting busier. Why we encourage illegal aliens to come here for jobs and welfare is beyond my comprehension.

The brightest future for us is agriculture and its demand from many countries grows by leaps and bounds. The other is American culture, like movies and music since English is, and will be, the most popular language. The recent discoveries in shale gas and oil are very promising. It could lead us to be a major energy exporter in the next 50 years. Military weapons are a big seller that I do not think it is good for the rest of the world.

Starting in 2012, the baby boomers are retiring (those who were born after the WW2). Hence, we will have about 20 years of increased entitlements such as Social Security considering the average life expectancy of about 82 years. Now we should have a boom in health care delivery.

- Japan.
  Japan does not have a lot of natural resources, and the educated citizen is their most important resource. Japan will suffer the most due to aging population. However, most of us will still drive a car from a Japanese company, play video game on Wii or PlayStation... Its competitors (now Korea and later China) will share their market. Japan will continue its lost decades to another decade. Japan seems turning around in 2013 but it could be just "the dead cat bounces". Only time can tell. Depreciating its currency further stimulates its export at least in the short term.

Conclusion

Investors should look at the sectors that will be benefitted from the aging population for the next 20 years. They are health care delivery, medical equipment, drugs, elderly housing and all sectors that cater to this growing age group.

Afterthoughts

More
http://ebmyth.blogspot.com/2013/11/more-on-aging-population.html

Links

Water re-directed.
http://en.wikipedia.org/wiki/South-North_Water_Diversion_Project

Ted Talk.
http://www.ted.com/talks/yasheng_huang.html

Filler:

16 EU's mess

We follow the similar procedure in finding the reentry points and use VGK, an ETF for European countries.

There are two sectors that bring down the financial crisis in 2007 (or 2008 for some). We should reenter the European market via technical analysis (TA) and via fundamental analysis.

Technical Analysis

There are two ways to find the reenter points after 2007.

1. Use the same chart in described in TA chapter as follows. Bring up Yahoo! And then Finance from the browser. Enter VGK, an ETF for Europe. Select Chart, then SMA (single moving average), and enter 350 days for reenter points (different from our usual 30, 60, 90 or 120 days).

   Loosely we have two major reenter/exit sets: 08/31/09 to 08/01/11 and 08/20/2012 to 01/13/14. Without considering compounding, we calculate the averages of these two sets of data.

2. From the Market Timing chapter, reenter the market 2 years after the initial plunge for offending sectors. They are not the offending sector but the sovereign debt is partly the culprit. Hence we use 18 months instead of 1 year for the general market or 2 years for the offending sector.

   Assuming 01/14/2008 the market starting plunging, the reenter date is 07/14/2009.

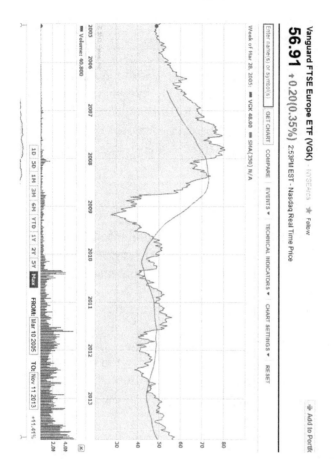

Source: Yahoo!Finance
(http://ebmyth.blogspot.com/2013/11/screen-vgk-350-day-sma.html)

The 350-day Single Moving Average could be a good guide to trade VGK, an ETF for European countries. Buy when it is above the moving average line and sell when it is below.

The following table summarizes the returns based on reenter points to 01/13/2014.

	Reenter Date	Return	Annualized Return	Beat SPY
Chart	08/10/09	-9%	-5%	-185%
	08/20/12	29%	21%	0%
Average		10%	8%	-93%

18 months	07/14/09	59%	13%	-42%

If you have a time machine, you may not want to invest in VGK at all as SPY beats both strategies by a wide margin. However, the annualized return is 8% and 13%, not too far away from XHB's 21% and 21% respectively. It seems Europe had more ups and downs during the recovery and the recovery is slower than the US market.

Fundamental analysis

Here are my personal thoughts as of 2009. I prefer to stick with the technical analysis and fundamental analysis is used to further analyze the housing market such as the cities that may have better recoveries. By the time you read this article, the information may be obsolete. Use it as a reference for future guidance.

As of 1/1/2012, my predication about EU's mess that we talked about more than two years ago (my blog mentioned it long before most media). Even today (9/2013), there are not a lot of changes and EU is still on its early stage to recovery. Here are my random remarks.

- EU will be dissolved or will at least kick out the cheaters, free loaders and parasites such as Greece. In any case, Euro will depreciate a lot compared to gold [Update as of 2013: It has]. Germany wants to keep Greece in the union despite of all the problems and little to gain. Germany have to compromise to the opposition from her own citizens in not giving up their own money.

- After that, a default is not a bad option.

- There will be conflicts in the citizens in Greece between those who have (still a lot collecting over $40,000 USD pension) and those (especially the young generation) who have to suffer due to passing the debts / miseries to them.

- Greece will recover faster if it has its own currency and it can default its debts. At that time, it would be profitable to invest in Greece.

Their government will be halved and the salaries / pension obligations will also be halved. To conclude, it will run the country about ¼ of the original cost. Tax revenues will come back with tourists looking for bargains. When the other industries such as shipping (when global trade improves) and processing olive return, the investment will have a good chance to gain 100% in a year. Timing is everything.

- The days living off from the treasures / commodities they stole from their colonies have been long, long gone. Most European countries need to live within their means.

- The lesson of having a good life without working hard (short work week and long vacation) is learned again and again. First it is Ireland, Iceland, then Greece, then Spain/Italy and now the USA.

- When they learn so many bitter lessons, they will not repeat them for a long while. The USA should learn the same lessons as we seem to be heading to the same direction unless the shale energy rescues us.

- EU will be a problem for years to come. When the country has that high debt with regard to GDP, they will not be competitive especially the drain of their best citizens to other countries.

- Decoupling is the solution. The U.S. and China will not be stupid or big enough to rescue a sinking ship.

Afterthoughts

- Update on Greece as of 1/2013.

Greece should be bottom out in a year. Investing in Greek stocks at that time would double your investment for the following reasons.

1. Greece is small, so it may not be a big deal to recover as Iceland did. It is better than Iceland with its nice climate and many attractions for tourists.

2. Besides attractions for tourists, Greece has beautiful beaches. They need to cut down protests before the tourists would return.

3. The government could be mean and small with about 1/4 of the previous expenses to run it.

4. The olive industry and the shipping industry will return big time after the global recession.

However, there are no cures for laziness and stupidity; another living proof on my Coconut Theory. The major hurdle is that there is a brain drain of able citizens and the retirees suck up the resources of the country.

- Roots of the problem.

1. Euro is initially a good idea especially for tourists. However, it forces the rich countries to pay for the free loaders.
2. Laziness is a human nature. When you work 30 hours (even less if you consider the long vacation) a week, you cannot compete with folks who work 50 hours a week.
3. The loots from the days being colonial masters were long gone except the displays in museums.
4. Socialism encourages folks to be parasites until the host dies.

Filler: The New Norm

Before I posted in Facebook, they asked me to select all the pictures of a lion. I skipped those pictures with two lions and they told me I was wrong. They need to hire someone graduated from high school.

They told me they're college graduates. Another sad day for our education system! Have you watched the movie "Idiocracy"? If you have, you understand what I mean.

Mediocrity is the new norm!?

17   The myths on China

"China as a sleeping lion whose roar would one day shake the world." - Napoleon.

Yes, China is roaring in this decade and the roar is getting louder and louder.

The most successful story in the last two decades

When the USA played the China card against Russia, it took away the embargo. Deng Xiaoping started an economic zone to build infrastructure (electricity, road, etc.) in an undeveloped city in South China and the rest is history. It is my Coconut Theory that when hard working folks have a chance to sell their 'coconuts', they will prosper. Lifting millions from starving to death is no small task. To me, Deng and Nixon should receive a Nobel Prize. However, since China has dominated the world, except the last three centuries, it is no surprise to me.

The Myths on China

Sam Walton was a patriot. He preferred to make less money by not selling Chinese goods. He estimated wrongly the profits from the Chinese products. When he died, the company turned into stores for Chinese products making his heirs the richest family and many of his investors millionaires.

Investors should not follow these myths that have been spread by TV networks and even professors.

- A TV network advocates "Made in USA" in a series.
- A professor from a prestigious university believed India will replace China as their population is younger.
- A professor from one of our top universities believed colonization is good using Hong Kong as an example.
- China is evil and they are communists.
- They're stealing our jobs, technologies and movies.
- All Chinese products are inferior products.

All the above are wrong or not totally correct and I will dispute them one by one.

Globalization

China is one country in the chain of the global economy which promotes free trade. Buy the best product from the country that produces the best product at the least cost. Globalization debunks the myths.

- China is moving up the product-value ladder. Some manufactured products, such as garments, will be moved to countries such as Vietnam and Burma with wages lower than China. This TV series makes you feel good and hence makes it easy for them to sell their advertising. In reality, manufacturing in many products will not come back to the USA due to our high wages, regulations and taxes. In a sentence, we're hurt by our own success. We need to give up these industries that we cannot possibly compete in and concentrate our efforts on high-value industries and industries we can compete in.
- Product quality is controlled by outsourcers. Do you find product quality problems in Apple's products?
- When you have a new technical product, you may want to assemble in South China, where most other OEMers such as cable and battery are available.
- In many cases we are copying China's mobile technology where China depends on.
- From 2013 to September, 2016, China has only one failed rocket launch. It is the cheapest and most reliable launch platform. We cannot use it due to security argument. However, it provides a good source for the space station that China is building one themselves. By 2025, China could be the only nation on earth that has a space station.
- China has never wanted to be number one. From Opium Wars to 30 years or so ago, China had been bullied by foreigners helping Brits pushing opium to China. China built the Great Wall to keep the invaders away. They could have colonized many countries in the 1400s, but they did not.
- China is not stealing our jobs, but globalization does. Most companies can outsource all functions of the company to other countries where they can find the best workers at the least costs.
- China is polluting the world. Aside from the pollution from factories producing products for export, energy consumption

per capita is far less than ours. China is #1 or #2 in most green energy technologies. Unfortunately, China is blessed with coal, but not blessed with the less-polluting gas and oil.

- China is stealing our movies and intellectual properties. It is the same for most developing countries. China will enforce intellectual properties before it can move up to the next phase to a developed country. Our companies have to protect our secrets as the best defense is a good offense. Even the US had been in that stage briefly. Charles Dickens was so angry that he did not want to visit the US. Did we pay royalty to Hitler for using German rocket technology and other similar technologies?

We can shut ourselves out from all foreign trades, but it will harm us more than help us. We have to enjoy a $50 toaster to start. All the chicken feet, a delicacy for the Chinese, will be dumped into the ocean. Our high-tech companies, farmers, movie industry will suffer.

Communism and China

China is only communist in the second "C" of CCP, China Communist Party. Chinese are more capitalist than us. If you do not work, you do not eat. This simple rule motivates its citizens to work hard. The safety net is improving, but it is a long way from our social security system; our system may be too generous as it has encouraged too many free loaders and cheaters (also in the corporation level too). It explains why they have a high savings rate. Most companies in China do not have unions, inconveniences of labor laws and sometimes even help from corrupt officials. After a taste of capitalism, China will never return to communism, which encourages folks to be lazy.

Human rights and Tibet

When you compare present day China to the China 30 years, 20 years or even 10 years ago, human rights have grown by leaps and bounds. To me, food and shelter come first before human freedom. Human freedom should be allowed gradually and it requires educated citizens that China has, except in the rural areas. Allowing freedom too fast would cause chaos (my thought and is debatable).

Before the 'liberation' of Tibet, only monks could get an education. One-child policy does not apply to Tibetans and other minorities. Their culture is maintained throughout from the experiences in my two visits in the last 10 years.

Hong Kong

Present and past, Hong Kong's wealth depends on its proximity to China, contrary to the colonialism theory a professor had stated. I had bet on the iShares MSCI Hong Kong ETF (NYSEARCA:EWH) (an ETF for Hong Kong) at the start of the Umbrella Protest. My order had not been executed due to my low price. The reason that the stock market did not drop further could be the plan allowing citizens in China and Hong Kong to buy stocks from the opposite exchanges. It will materialize soon after they finalize the tax and regulation details. Hence, the Chinese have more investment choices instead of investing in ghost cities.

India

Indians compare themselves with the Chinese, but the Chinese usually compare themselves with the USA. India will not catch up with China in this decade. It is more corrupt than China, more protective than China, and has more social inequality than China. The Tier I cities in India cannot compete with the Tier II cities in China when you compare the infrastructure, high rises, subway, airport, etc.

The growing population of India eats up all the limited resources of the country. As a Chinese saying goes, you get rich by making fewer babies and building more roads.

China's advantages

- Huge internal market. The scale of economies is quite obvious.
- An educated and hard-working work force.
- Relatively low wages for qualified engineers and researchers. The wage of one US engineer is about the same as four Chinese engineers from my rough estimate. It is giving some technology companies problems, such as Cisco.
- Government incentives and subsidies.

- Most big projects and major purchases to foreign countries have a clause of technology transfer. If we do not oblige, they buy them from your competitor. The trick is to use the money for research (not bonuses to the management) and hold out the top technology.
- Bitter tough lessons in the past 300 years starting from the Opium Wars to WW2.
- One-party political system is not a bad thing. By the time China connects most, if not all, the Tier I cities with high speed trains, we're still arguing about who is on top for the first one.

The success of China is good to the world

After the last earthquake struck China, Chinese and the overseas Chinese helped to rebuild the disaster region without asking other nations for help. If China is as poor as before, you may have 20% of the world population begging for money.

When you need a drug to cure a terminal disease, do you care whether it is from the USA or from China?

It has rescued many US companies such as GM from bankruptcy. So is Volvo. China will buy many bankrupted US companies if we allow them. Some bankrupted US companies do not have much salvage values, but we argue not to sell on national security reason. Most do not make sense.

Vietnam is copying China's model and it is at least 15 years behind. Eventually, many factory jobs will be replaced by robots and countries such as Vietnam with labor cost even far lower than China. Our politicians have to WAKE up and try to solve our problems instead of blaming our problems on China. It already has attracted many industries such as textile that cannot afford the rising wages in China. The latest riot against foreign factories (mostly from Taiwan) is more political and not against the Chinese. The Chinese have been more integrated with the Vietnamese than most other SE Asian countries.

Resource-rich countries such as Brazil and Australia benefit from the demand in China. They will return to the normal trade levels when the global economy improves. Macau and Hong Kong have been benefiting from Chinese tourists. With the suppression of corruption, the gambling industry in Macau will suffer. Due to the recent Umbrella Protest, Hong Kong will suffer from fewer Chinese tourists.

China has become number one in tourist spending in France. It is similar to many other countries. Most companies producing luxury products benefit. The myth of an average Chinese citizen making less than $5,000 is debunked by these tourists. Firstly, the median salary is not $5,000 and secondly the size of the middle class is huge. Most countries benefit with the rise of China today, except Japan, which has an islet dispute with China. Philippines, backed up by the USA, has similar problems with China. Hope they will resolve the problem by sharing resources.

Not too long we will compete with China on higher-value products as we're competing with Western Europe now. There are many recent examples that worry me more. A Chinese company captures 70% market of the consumer drone that was invented by our military. Chinese military drones cost about one quarter of ours and they have little restrictions to whom they sell to. Chinese has a monster machine to build bridges. They have more than the high-speed rail than all other countries combined. These are a few of many examples. If we ignore Chinese products due to poor quality, then we may have lived in a cave for the last year. When the average Chinese student spends at least two more hours in studying than ours, they will achieve more in life and catch up fast.

Afterthoughts

Being born in Hong Kong, I am naturally biased. I try to present this article with facts. China has a lot of problems that most developing countries have.

The following data are obtained from Barron's article dated on Nov. 17. 2014.

	Vietnam	Cambodia	Laos	Thailand	Myanmar
GDP Growth	5%	7%	8%	3%	8%
Export Growth	12%	13%	17%	0%	16%
Population	93 M	16 M	7 M	68 M	56 M
Monthly MFG Wage	$250	$130	$140	$370	$110
ETF	VNM			THD	

Thailand is the most developed with a thriving tourist industry. However, political unrest would take it several steps back. This article is dedicated to our beloved Boston mayor Thomas Menino 1942-2014. This article was published in Seeking Alpha on 11-2014, a site for investors.

http://seekingalpha.com/article/2644635-debunk-the-myths-on-china

Learn more on China

Geography   https://www.youtube.com/watch?v=lzAESaVqix0

History   *(about 250 BC on & simplified)*
https://www.youtube.com/watch?v=yIP9jR4JHw4

My music *selection*
http://tonyp4idea.blogspot.com/2016/07/chinese-music.html
D20 Showtime
https://www.youtube.com/watch?v=GeeDUDhMOs
Chinese space *program* https://en.wikipedia.org/wiki/Chinese_space_program
Tai Chi
https://www.youtube.com/watch?v=_FKKjWl1-OU

18   The states of the United States

Contrary to popular belief, we DO make and build something especially per capita wise. We're still the largest economy on earth and are number one in most disciplines in science and technology. We have a stable government with an enviable constitution, workable regulations, highly-educated citizens and the strongest defense (or offense to me).

Our government and the private citizens (Gates and Buffett for example) donate funds and assistance to poor countries more than the other five richest countries combined. We provide food to the world. We export our culture via movies and music. We accept foreign students to enrich our culture, fund our colleges, and provide us with skilled workers when they graduate.

We have a lot of innovations such as Facebook. Most of our products have high profit margins such as airplanes, heavy equipment, high tech products including Apple's consumer products and medical equipment. Nobody can deny that.

Our success leads to higher living standard. Naturally the higher labor cost and more regulations to protect us and our environment follow. Too many regulations would restrict businesses in taking risks (such as developing new drugs and nuclear reactor technologies) and add costs to product developments.

We have to leave the low-end products to low-wage countries such as China. It is called free trade and globalization, which would benefit all participants if they play the game fairly. China's 1.35 billion citizens would not be able to buy our expensive products if they do not have the cash from selling their products to the world.

We have to protect those products that we have an edge. It is not an easy job just by comparing the quality of our high school education to the rest of the world. Japan and S. Korea have passed us in auto and consumer electronic industries. China is at the gate with bigger impact in the future. China is catching up with us. In addition, it has a large internal market, plenty of qualified engineers / scientists, low-wage workers and incentives / guidance from the government. The most important is their desire and spirit to succeed after three centuries of humiliation.

God still blesses us with the new discoveries of shale energy that could extend our prosperity to another 50 years. It gives us more time to fix our problems, but time is running out. The benefits of the shale energy will be clearer by 2015. It could turn out to be a pure fantasy or even a sham. We are still a net natural gas importer (most from Canada) and our gas industry is currently sitting on heavy losses.

Compared to China, we have far, far more farm land and natural resources especially per capita wise.

Our welfare system is too generous due to our previous economic booms. If the able welfare recipients lose the free medical care for taking a job, do they work? They're lazy but not stupid. With the long dependence on this welfare system, they cannot break the viscous cycle of poverty. Multi generation of teenage mothers is one among many examples.

The new immigration bill could be a disaster. If it is passed, how many new legal residents will collect welfare (they can't today as they're illegal) and how many illegals are encouraged to cross the defenseless border. I hope the new immigrants will contribute more than burden our society. Only time can tell. However, protecting the border is easy by severely punishing the employers. When there are no jobs, they will not come. The USA is still the best country for immigrates.

There are many frauds and fats that the government can trim. The government employees are assigned to tiny work load and they are overly compensated. Should we assign them to chase after the frauds in Medicare, food stamp and cheatings in disability entitlements that are so common?

The two wars are bankrupting this country and we need to prevent starting future wars and end the current wars. As of 2013, our military budget is larger than the total of the next top five countries combined.

From this article, you know the government can fix a lot of our problems. Printing money is not the solution, but the problem by itself.

We need to encourage productivity and discourage consumption. Buying a car is consumption and building a bridge is improving productivity. Welfare to the able poor is consumption and teaching work skills to the poor is improving productivity that leads to production increase.

What worries me most is: We're declining while many developing countries (China in particular) are surging up.

The future will be decided by our high school system which is falling apart. Our society is too permissive from gun controls to legalizing drugs, which may bring infant defects. Our lawyers sue every one for profit no matter how ridiculous the cases are.

Solutions are quite simple

To summarize, we should cut most expenses and balance the budget. It is hard to implement as most do not want to bit the bullet. We're a nation of free loaders with over 40% not working.

1. No illegals to legal. When they become legal, they will collect welfare legally and bring their families in for the same reason.

2. Train and encourage the able welfare recipients to work. Cutting their benefits in taking a job will not encourage them to work. Clinton's Initiative has more holes than Swiss cheese.

3. Cut down our generous welfare. That's why we have three generations of teen age mothers. Laziness is a human nature.

4. End the endless wars. If they do not want to fight for their own freedom, why should we (suckers in their eyes)?

5. We cannot borrow forever and pass our debts to next generations. USD will not be a reserve currency in 10 years. Printing money excessively is a short-term solution but a problem long-term problem.

6. Invest in our infrastructure.

7. Cut down foreign aids. A big brother is only in the mind of our leaders.

8. We need a small and efficient government. Guard changing when another party takes over is expensive.

Afterthoughts

- Will the new immigrants strengthen our society?
  http://www.americanprogress.org/issues/immigration/news/2012/12/10/47406/progressive-immigration-policies-will-strengthen-the-american-economy/

- Immigration reform will likely depress the average wage over the next 10 years, according to the Congressional Budget Office and also will likely increase our burden in our welfare and entitlement systems.

- Paul said:
  This WAS a country where government did not buy votes. When my grandparents came to the U.S., there were no Federal social programs, no Social Security, no Medicare, no welfare and no income taxes. Millions poured into this country looking for opportunity -- not a safety net...

- From ZeroHedge: (http://www.zerohedge.com/)
  The only recovery you'll see this summer is after a night of heavy drinking...

  Nothing has changed since 2008, nobody was arrested, no laws put in place, nobody held accountable. We all know that companies like JP Morgan and Goldman Sachs bundled toxic sub-prime mortgages into securities and paid off the ratings agencies to rate them AAA then bet against them using CDS with companies like AIG. So what does the government do? Reward their criminal and fraudulent behavior by completely bailing them out and then giving them oodles of cheap credit.

- The government needs to encourage folks and/or train them to work. Raising minimum wage is making the problem worse. The government should encourage businesses to stay in the USA and not to tax the very rich excessively.

- My recent blogs.
  My update. http://tonyp4idea.blogspot.com/2014/08/good-deeds-and-bad-deeds.html

  Immigration and Racism.
  http://tonyp4idea.blogspot.com/2014/08/immigration-and-racisim.html

  Legalized drugs.
  http://tonyp4idea.blogspot.com/2014/08/drug-kills.html

  The Constitution.
  http://tonyp4idea.blogspot.com/2014/08/change-constitution.html

Links:
Military budgets:
http://247wallst.com/2013/06/27/countries-spending-the-most-on-the-military/?link=mktw

Filler

*** iPhone & drones ***

Almost 100% of drones are made in China. Should we check whether the Chinese have back doors in the drones? They could instruct the drones to take pictures or just use them to kill everything that moves. Hope it is a joke.

VI Strategy 6: Asset class

It includes house, oil, commodities and precious metals.

19   Market timing by asset class

Two major trading strategies are:

1. Buy high and sell higher.
    It is a kind of momentum play. You may keep these stocks for less time (say, less than three months). The momentum could change very fast. In my momentum portfolio, I keep most of my stocks not more than a month.

2. Buy low and sell high.
    When the asset class is totally out-of-favor and it has high value, buy. It is a value play. You are swimming against the tide. You need to hold these stocks longer (say, longer than 6 months) for the market to realize its value.

It is not possible to predict correctly the peaks and bottoms of any asset class consistently. However, #1 usually starts first and followed by #2. The holding period is just a suggestion.

Your success will be improved by using Technical Analysis correctly. Try the 60-day moving average to start. Buy when it is above the average and sell when it is below. Next, try the 30-day moving average and many other technical analysis indicators such as exponential moving average and different days for the moving averages. Basically there is a tradeoff on switching too frequently and reacting too lately.

Try out different asset classes such as gold and oil. To illustrate, no one can predict that gold price at $1800 is the peak. If you buy coin coins at $1000 and ride the gold wagon to $1600, you're doing quite well. However, the gold price at $1000 could be interpreted as the peak unless you have a time machine. ☺

My experience in gold

I had gold coins at about $400 each. Gold did not appreciate much for over 20 years. When its price rose to $800, I sold some. I made 100% return, but it did not even beat inflation. If I invested in stocks instead of gold coins, I would be far better off especially with dividends. When gold rose to $1000, I sold more. Our rational thinking (part of human nature) would not allow us to hold these coins until 1,800. The moral is no one can predict the peak value of an asset and act accordingly.

Trading coins in your local shops would take a lot of commission even if it is safer to do so. The coin shops will not report your sales to IRS if the sell is below a certain amount as of 2011. Check the current rule.

Afterthoughts

- A case of 'Buy High and Sell Higher' or 'Buy High and Sell Low'.

  Today 8/6/13, my buy order on TA was executed in the morning after the earnings conference. The stock plunged about 30%. The lessons are:

  o The stock was up to $12 form $3 in last two years. It has appreciated a lot already. I should avoid this stock as I prefer 'Buy Low and Sell High' strategy.

  o Should have checked the recent earnings revisions. It has not scored well in this aspect. I have ignored this indicator that is available in one of my subscriptions.

  o It is still a value stock. The stock price has been priced in. When the earning does not meet the expected, it plunges.

20   Housing recovery?

There are two sectors (housing finance) that caused the financial crisis in 2007 (or 2008 for some). We should reenter the housing market via technical analysis (TA) and via fundamental analysis.

Technical Analysis

There are two ways to find the reenter points after 2007.

1. Use the same chart in described in TA chapter as follows. Bring up Yahoo! And then Finance from the browser. Enter XLB, an ETF for housing construction. Select Chart, then SMA (single moving average), and enter 350 days for reenter points (different from our usual 30, 60, 90 or 120 days).

   There are 2 or 3 exit points and followed by brief reenter points. They are noises and they do not change the final performance.

2. From the Market Timing chapter, reenter the market 2 years after the initial plunge for offending sectors (they are Finance and Construction for 2007). Assuming 10/12/07 the market starting plunging, the reenter date is 10/12/09.

The following table summarizes the returns based on reenter points to 01/13/2014.

	Reenter Date	Return	Annualized Return	Beat SPY
Chart	08/10/2009	95%	21%	15%
2 Year	10/12/2009	89%	21%	30%

The Chart method makes more money but the annualized return is the same. However, the '2-Year' strategy beats SPY 100% better than the Chart strategy.

Fundamental analysis

Here are my personal thoughts as of 2009. I prefer to stick with the technical analysis and fundamental analysis is used to further analyze the housing market such as the cities that may have better recoveries. By the time you read this article, the information may be obsolete. Use it as a reference for future guidance.

- Location.
  NYC does not lose a lot in housing values. Las Vegas, many cities in Florida and sunny area does. Cities that are going to bankrupt such as Detroit and a few cities in California are great bargain but too risky.

  A well-maintained house in a good neighborhood at 2002 price is a good bargain when you compare to build the same house with both increased material cost and eventually labor cost. You may get a newer and modern house, but the location is usually better and is less pricy.

- Inventory still high.
  We do not have a lot of building since 2008. The inventory is very low now but some banks are still holding a lot of foreclosed properties and properties that should be foreclosed. Some properties are in very bad shape and they should be demolished.

- Who drives the housing market.
  If we have a W-shaped recession and/or a lost decade similar to Japan's, the housing recovery will take longer than two years. The builders will be profitable if they can manage their resources and projects on smaller houses for today's smaller and / or less affluent families and more elderly housing for the aging population.

  One of the major forces that trigger the housing boom is the college graduates. When they have children, it is time to buy a house. It does not look good today as most are under-employed or unemployed with large college loans. The U.S. economy may recover without job recovering. Many jobs have been outsourced and most lost jobs will not return. The rosiest sector is energy. We may have 2.5 million new jobs in this sector in 3 years. The house prices in these selected cities skyrocket.

Are today's houses affordable? You can afford a house costing 2 ½ of your yearly income. I would use 3 times today especially with the low interest rates and today's rent alternative. As of 5/2013, the basic housing is on the cheap side for potential buyers especially for those who are still employed and it will remain so as long as the interest rate remains low.

Interest rate.
The housing market depends on interest rate more than most other industries. Low interest rates would make housing more affordable. That's what happened in June, 2013 when the interest rate moved up from the bottom and the housing recovery came to a halt.

I bet the interest rate would be less a factor when the economy is fully recovered.

- Foreigner purchase is the key.
  On the bright side, there are foreigners (a lot from China and some with money from questionable sources) want to buy them in cash. Finally we encourage rich immigrants who invest in the US. It also helps a lot of corrupt officials to escape prosecution by buying residency in the US. Some initial purchases have lost more than 25% of their investment, but some later ones have experienced more than 100% return. Timing is everything!

Compared to Hong Kong and most big cities in China, the US houses are bargains. Many cost about half a million to buy a 500 square feet apartment in a desirable area compared to some 3000-square feet mansions (relative to 500 square feet) in Southern states.

The quality in life is far better here in terms of air quality, water quality, food quality, education (ease to go to colleges) and opportunities.

Most Chinese and many Asians do not buy a house with street number 4 (pronounced 'dead' in Chinese) and bad Feng Shui that many sellers in Vancouver and Toronto have found out. Cities with better culture and well-known colleges such as

Boston attract rich foreigners sending their children there. When I was in NYC, I (and 1.3 billion Chinese) would tell you Pam Am Building had bad Feng Shui as the road was running through the building. There are some locations where businesses fell one after. I can explain most are due to very bad Feng Shui. I am not superstitious, but good Feng Shui provides a relaxing living place.

Afterthoughts

- Is the recent (1/2013) rise in housing stocks justified? There are two camps of opposing arguments. Only time can tell which one is right.

  For the low housing inventory and the slowly improving economy, it could be time to buy on construction stocks and REITs (especially the hospital REITs but not the REITs on mortgages). The recent recovery could be temporary due to lower inventory and the interest rate is climbing.

- If you believe the housing will be recovered soon and you do not want to buy specific construction stocks, try the ETF XHB.

- The housing market is irrational. 'Buy Low and Sell High' applies here. From an economist as of 5/2013: Comparing to rents and incomes, the overall housing market is still under-valued by Rabout 7% from the bottom of 15%. It was over-valued by about 40% in 2006.

- Before the takeover of Hong Kong by China, Vancouver properties doubled in values very fast. It is happening in some cities in the US by Chinese buyers this time. However, we do not see this effect here as Vancouver is small compared to the entire USA. It is a double-edged sword. The sellers are happy and the potential local buyers are not as they have to compete with foreigners who pay more and in cash.

- The average house has been increased excessively since 2000. As many times in this book, excessive valuation will bring down to the average value. Compare to Hong Kong and most big cities in China, our houses are still underpriced.

Depending on which yardstick you're using, you get different conclusions. The better one should be: The average house price should not be more than three times the average annual income.

- I remember Uncle Ben told us not to worry and four months later the housing market crashed. Cheat me twice, shame on me.

- When the economy returns, there will be more jobs and more folks buying homes. It is good for the housing sector. It even beats out the disadvantage of the higher interest rate, which is no longer needed to be lowered to stimulate the economy.

- Learn from mistakes.
  He made several mistakes as every investor did. He sold the businesses in re-insurance, airline, etc. but he seldom made the same mistake again. Learn from how he deals with his mistakes.

- He does not follow hot fad such as the internet in 2000. I prefer to follow it, but have an exit plan and protect profits.

- Evaluate stocks with common sense. Mathematical models on stocks are for professors to have a job and they never resemble real life.

- Buffett has switched between bonds and stocks successfully. Most of the time, he was not the first one to exit, but he adapted to the market conditions better than most of us. He usually pays more than the market and/or bottom prices but it has turned out many times he was right.

- Buffett as a person has a lot for us to learn from. He is frugal and generous. Making money is his career and hobby, not because he loves to make money for worldly stuffs. For that, he should go to heaven one day.

- Buffett has his share of bad investing decisions such as buying IBM instead of buying Google, Microsoft and Apple. Do not bet the entire farm in one deal.

- According to Buffett and Peter Lynch, they had been misled more often than getting meaningful information by calling CEOs. In addition, most of us cannot even reach anyone important.

Filler:

A report card

According to Cruz, all politicians should have a report card to see what his/her campaign ideas/promises have been fulfilled. I'm political neutral. The words are wise and can it be enforceable?

Simple concept, but big impact.

21   Commodities: bottom or mirage?

Most authors reveal a statement first and then illustrate with examples to substantiate that statement. Hence, such writers are always right. I am doing something just the opposite in this article. In analyzing what coal stocks to buy (the example) and you help me to verify the bottom for coal stocks (the statement).

This process has its risks, as I try to emphasize that investing is a prediction, which will not be 100% certainty. However, the better educated the guesses are, the better chances the predictions will be materialized. Even if that prediction is wrong, there is nothing wrong with the logic here.

Actually the recommended stocks should be bought in the future as it may not be the bottom today (7/4/13). Confusing? Read on.

Several articles convince me that commodity especially coal should be close to the bottom. Here are the links to these articles. That's the reason why you want to read economic news to take advantage of any new opportunity.

1. The coming rebound of coal and coal stocks.
    http://seekingalpha.com/article/1530202-the-coming-rebound-in-commodities-coal-and-coal-stocks

2. A credit analysis of coal mining companies.
    http://seekingalpha.com/article/1509622-a-credit-analysis-for-coal-mining-companies

Is the bottom near for commodities?

For the last three years, the bottoms of coals stocks have been predicted several times. Nevertheless the coal stocks went up temporarily and then continued its bearish trend. Many coal companies could go bankrupt. I bet most of them will not and offer one of the best appreciation potential, but I do not go that far to proclaim it is one of the best deals in our generation.

Many experts believe natural gas would replace coal to generate electricity. The impact of natural gas will be even clearer by 2016. That may be true in the USA, but not in China and many countries.

Even with all the nuclear generators on-line in ten years (2023), China will still depend on coal to generate more than 60% of its electricity.

The following tables may not look good on small screens. You can enter the link below to display it on a larger screen of your PC.

(http://ebmyth.blogspot.com/2013/07/screens-on-commodity-chapter.html)

The stocks

I include 15 stocks and one ETF for analysis. After the initial analysis, I classify them into the following groups.

	Coal	Gold miner ETF	General Mining	Steel	Petroleum w Nat Gas
No.	11	1	1	1	2
Stock	ACI,ANR,ARLP, BTU,CLD,CNX, JRCC,NRP, WLB,WLT, YZC	GDX	RIO	SID	CHK,DVN

Value

These stocks have very high potential for appreciation. However, they are risky. Nothing risked, nothing gained. Most have high debts (the average debt/equity is 133% in this group) and their survival depends on many factors such as the prices of the commodities. The following table concentrates on their values.

Stock	Price (7/4/13)	Forward Yield	Cash Flow	P/B	Debt/ Equity	P-Score
ACI	3.69	-35%	Worst	.3	184%	-4
ANR	5.33	-75%	Worst	.2	70%	-6
ARLP	71.06	10%	Average	3.6	109%	8
BTU	14.86	3%	Worst	.8	126%	-2
CHK	20.92	5%	Worst	1.1	106%	1
CLD	16.19	5%	Worst	1.0	83%	-2
CNX	27.12	10%	Worst	1.6	81%	-1

DVN	53.05	5%	Worst	1.1	82%	-2
JRCC	1.82	-80%	Worst	.3	255%	-5
NRP	20.48	10%	Average	3.4	172%	3
RIO	40.69	10%	Average	1.6	57%	0
SID	2.61	15%	Worst	5.6	329%	2
WLB	11.4	5%	Best			-1
WLT	10.79	-35%	Worst	.5	276%	-2
YZC	7.03	15%	Best	.5	90%	4

BTU has coal mines in Australia, which is closer to its primary customer, China. RIO has mines of different ores all over the world. ARLP and NRP are partnerships.

If you do not want to deal with extra effort in filing the tax returns, buy partnerships in a non-taxable account. I have not checked out the requirements for filing tax returns for ARLP and NRP.

GDX, an ETF for gold miners, is not included in the above table. It has a huge non-correlation between GLD, the ETF for gold, so I believe there is good value in gold miners. GDXJ (not included in this article) is a similar one for junior miners, which is too risky for me.

Most data are obtained from finviz.com. Forward yield is my estimate and it is defined as forward E/P. Cash Flow is based on the free site Blue Chip Growth. Cash Flow and Debt / Equity measure whether the company will survive. The table does not include all the metrics. P-Score is based on my book Scoring Stocks and 3 is the passing grade.

I have two scoring systems. One is described in my book Scoring Stocks and the other one uses information from several subscription services. In general, the two systems are quite compatible. When the commodities are in the market bottom, the scores for these stocks would not be good. Actually most of them do not pass (the passing grade is 3).

YZC scores the highest and it has the high dividend yield.

ACI and ANR though risky have the most upside potential and both prices are less than 30% of their book values.

Risk levels

The following table summarizes how safe are the stocks.

	Safer	Middle	Risky
No.	3	6	7
Stocks	ARLP, NRP, YZC	CHK, BTU, GDX, RIO, SID, WLB	ACI, ANR, CLD, CNX, DVN, JRCC, WLT

My contradiction

I contradict myself in the following statements.

1. I do not trust the financial sheet of emerging countries including China. However, when many miners are foreign companies, I do not have a good option.

2. Mining is a sector I try to avoid.
   It is extremely difficult to estimate how much ores (sometimes a miner owns several different ores of different grades in same or different mines) the company has; complicated by the complexities to extract and transport them. When those costs are greater its production price, the company will not be profitable. Understanding the market for ore futures is another discipline.

   One potential problem of mining companies from many emerging countries is nationalization.

Timing

Besides ARLP, NRP and YZC as of 7/4/2013, I would select the following to purchase after another analysis in Nov. 1, 2013: CHK, BTU, GDX, RIO, SID and WLB. I would skip the worst scored stocks, which are too risky for me but they may have the highest appreciation. ACI and ANR are very tempting though.

Why November? Most of these stocks have been down for the year and there is more pressure to sell them for window dressing for fund managers in Nov. (even earlier) and for tax write-offs for retail investors in Dec.

Technical analysis will not detect the bottom, but the trend. When the trend is up, the risk is less but the opportunity to buy at the bottom is gone. Today, the trends of most of these stocks are down. I will explore whether there is a correlation of the bottom with the percentage from the last peak.

Timing is a suggestion and you buy the stocks at your own risk and risk tolerance.

My plunge into commodities

I could not resist and bought two stocks from the above list. As of 8/9/13, the performances are quite good.

Stocks	Buy Date	Return	Annualized return
BTU	06/24/13	18%	140%
GDX	07/15/13	14%	150%
FCX	07/31/13	21%	850%
DBC	08/08/13	2%	Too early
NGD	09/12/13	14%	Too early

FCX is too good a price to pass and the insiders bought many shares. Annualized returns usually have no meaning when the holding period is less than 30 days. The annualized return is calculated by the formula: Return * 365 / (days between the buy date and today's date). For example, the annualized return for FCX = 21% * 365 (8-9-13 minus 7-31-13). The 850% return is not sustainable.

The return of DBC, an ETF for commodities, is tracked today 8/12/13. The above are actual and verifiable trades from my largest account. NGD, a gold miner, is added most recently and the return is calculated on 9/18/2013.

[Update: as of 9/6/13, the returns are: 20% for BTU, 21% for GDX, 8% for FCX and 5% for DBC.]

Conclusion

The coal stocks have the highest potential for appreciation, but they are also the riskiest. By spreading out the risk with having more than one coal stock and stay with the first group or by purchasing an ETF on coal stocks such as KOL. The ETF included here is for gold miners.

Catching the bottom of a sector is risky but could be very profitable. I believe it will take at least two years for the market to recognize the potential upside values of coal stocks. Several of these stocks may not survive. That also depends on the impact from the shale energy and the recovery of the economy.

Repeatedly, we the retail investors never learn the following lessons:

1. Buy in fears and sell in greed instead of the other way round.

2. All inflated sector (and deflated sector in this case) will return to the average value with only one or two exceptions. Gold in 2011 is not really an exception but the USD had been depreciated.

These two lessons are the cornerstones on how bubbles are formed / burst and how we can profit from the bottoms of these sectors.

Afterthoughts

*   Mike said:
    Thermal coal is dead for countries like the U.S. If you want thermal coal, buy foreign, like Yanzhou Coal Mining (YZC). China is not going to give up coal anytime soon. Plus, graph says the stock is at support http://yhoo.it/168vHaa;c=. And 7% dividend looks attractive. Metallurgical coal, which is used in steel making, will be what keeps coal alive in the U.S. (ANR) is a metallurgical coal miner.

*   Market Vectors Coal ETF (KOL).

- Bill said:
    1. I like KOL as a diversified play. Having said that, I don't think it will perform as strongly as some of the undervalued U.S. mining companies like ANR, ACI, WLT, BTU, and CNX.

    2. Coal stocks rallied strongly from their 2009 lows to their 2011 highs while Obama was in office. This is easy to forget. Ultimately, the political dialogue certainly has an impact, but I think the underlying economic fundamentals are by far the most important factor affecting the stock prices.

       Domestically, I think the historically warm 2011/2012 winter in the U.S., which was a short-term event, dramatically impacted the perception surrounding both coal and natural gas. It "amplified" fears and hopes. As inventories for both natural gas and coal normalize, which they have largely done, I think we will get a better view of both industries.

- I wrote an article on Rare Earth that was quite ahead of its time then. Most information is still valid.
  http://www.tonyp4idea.blogspot.com/2011/03/rare-earth.html

  This article was published in Seeking Alpha.
  http://seekingalpha.com/article/1817642-commodities-bottom-or-mirage

Links

Finviz:
http://www.finviz.com/

Scoring stocks:
http://www.amazon.com/Scoring-stocks-adaptive-scoring-Investing/dp/1484159330/

Blue Chip Growth:

http://navelliergrowth.investorplace.com/bluechip/password/index.php?plocation=%2Fbluechip%2F

China and coal:
http://www.forbes.com/sites/pikeresearch/2013/06/24/chinas-coal-conundrum/

From Wikipedia.
http://en.wikipedia.org/wiki/Coal_in_China

No peak for China.
http://www.forbes.com/sites/pikeresearch/2013/06/24/chinas-coal-conundrum/

Clean coal technology.
Carbon capture and higher efficient turbine.
http://tech.fortune.cnn.com/2013/01/08/a-bright-spot-in-chinas-coal-binge/

Coal and the US policy.
http://money.cnn.com/2013/07/03/news/economy/obama-coal/index.html?iid=HP_LN

Updated information on specific companies:
To illustrate, bring up SeekingAlpha.com and enter BTU. There should be several recent articles on BTU.

Here is one of the many articles on BTU.
http://seekingalpha.com/article/1533542-peabody-energy-commodity-contrarian-investing-101

The fair price of oil

Oil will not run out at least in our generation especially with the new-found shale energy. However, peak oil has come and passed. The easy oil (closer to the surface and lighter) is getting scarcer. The heavy oil, the oil from the ocean and the shale oil (depending on the region) are more expensive to extract.

As of 1/2015, the fair price of oil to me is $85 (down from $95 two years ago). It is due to the abundance of shale oil and the slow demand in a poor global economy. When the production cost is over $80 (today it is about $65), it will not be profitable for many productions (the difference of $5 is for profit). As of 1/2015, there are two camps: 1. Believe the oil price will drop below $60 (from today's $65) and 2. Believe the oil price will return above $80 soon.

I believe it will be back above $80 in a year. Many operations such as from oil sand to produce oil at the current price will not be profitable even in my optimistic prediction.

For this year, I would stay away from drillers and explorers and I am picking up those oil companies that have good expected P/E, low debts and have the production facilities to produce oil at around $80 per barrel. Even with all the safety measures, they're still risky buy for my predicted oil price at $85. However, the potential appreciation could be huge.

I expect there will be higher demand due to the higher living standard in China and India, and the larger global population. It is also higher due to the depreciation of USD and inflation. Hence, we need to adjust its fair price every six months or so.

OPEC would like to maintain the oil price at about $100 at today's USD for longer-term profit. Every country within OPEC has its own agenda, political issues and economic issues and they most likely would not consistently agree on a specific price.

However, when oil is higher than $125 for a long time in today's dollar, the alternative energies will be more feasible economically and conservation becomes more important. If oil price is a run-away to $150, we'll have another recession and that would bring the price back to the normal range. Economy adjusts the oil price to some extent and sometimes works better than OPEC.

Oil price has been fluctuating a lot in the last five years. It is purely due to speculation. The ease of money should cause inflation and inflates the oil price in particular. QE2 played a role, and so would be QEn if it will be materialized. The current restrictions in speculating commodities reduce the speculating on oil and could be the reason why oil price drops even with better economic outlook.

I do not trade oil unless it is priced to either extreme. When it was $35 per barrel, it was time to buy. When it was $140, it was time to sell. Adjust the numbers to today's dollar. It is an example of "Buy Low and Sell High". As of 1/2013, for the past 10 years, oil has an annualized return of 2.6% while inflation is 2.4%. The average return is negative after taxes and inflation. Unless you've a keen eye on oil, do not speculate on it. If you do, try the ETF Oil.

The biggest threat on oil and its producing countries is shale energy. From my prediction on 2/2013, oil price would rise until the shale energy will solve its extraction and transportation problems. At that time, oil prices would be under $100 in today's dollar for years to come [as of 1/2015, the oil price is about $65].

Retail investors should stick on fundamentals: Buy low and sell high.

Afterthoughts

- The real competitor to oil is shale gas and the shale oil. The U.S. has found enough to supply the country for the next 50 years. We have to see how the events such as pipeline construction and environment damages are being developed.

- Some believe all the US interventions in the Middle East, including the recent turmoil in N. Africa and the counter attacks, are due to oil and its transportation to the U.S. At one time we only enforced no-fly zone on countries that have oil. If so, shame on us. If it is the modern Crusade, shame on us in misinterpreting religions' preaching and the Congress which is controlled by Israel.

If we have enough shale oil and shale gas, we do not need to protect the oil route and we should have a peaceful world.

- Oil prices are moved short term by traders, midterm by expectation and longer term by supply and demand.

- GLD is an ETF similar to OIL with a different commodity. I wonder where they store the physical gold for GLD. Most likely they use derivatives. If so, it reminds of the derivatives created by Lehman Brothers.

- The price of every commodity is defined by supply and demand. When the global economy improves, prices of most industrial commodities will increase.

- The impact of China due to the improvement of their economy cannot be ignored. It will drive up the demand of most commodities – India to a smaller extent. Per capita wise, they still use far less commodities than the U.S. citizens after deducting the resources to build trinkets for export. However, their population is about 4 times larger than the U.S.

- To summarize as of 6/2013, commodities prices are affected by 2 major factors:

  1. The USD. If we use a basket of commodities to measure the value of USD. A decrease in value of the USD will increase the commodities prices. The USD has been in a temporary peak.

  2. Supply and demand. With poor global economies and the slowing down of China's internal growth (infrastructure and building...), the demand of industrial and construction commodities are decreasing and so are the prices. However, the US housing market is starting to boom (it could be a mirage and/or due to the shrinking inventory).

  There are many other minor factors such as speculation...

- Unimaginable not too long ago, the U.S. will be the largest energy producer by 2017, according to IEA, but a net exporter by 2030 and energy independent by 2035.

- My view as of 1/2015. No one (except God and the Middle East terrorists) can really predict the short-term direction of oil correctly. However, the long-term direction is clear. It will be up. When? One year, two years or three years. I can tell you exactly "when" when I fix my time machine.

Links

Click here for a similar article.
http://seekingalpha.com/article/975661-how-oil-really-gets-priced

Peak Oil:
http://en.wikipedia.org/wiki/Peak_oil

Energy boom?
http://finance.yahoo.com/blogs/the-exchange/play-america-energy-boom-160057023.html

Bottom for commodities?
http://seekingalpha.com/article/1530202-the-coming-rebound-in-commodities-coal-and-coal-stocks?v=1372760509&source=tracking_notify

A list of commodity ETFs:
http://etfdb.com/type/commodity/all/

Direction indicator of gold
price.http://seekingalpha.com/article/2374965-8-indicators-that-tell-us-where-gold-might-go-next

There are many articles on both camps predicting the oil price in SeekingAlpha.com. Here is one.

Falling oil price as of 1/2016

The oil price has been plunged to $28.76 (even lower several days ago) per barrel today. Trade OIL, an ETN (for simplicity treat it as ETF) stimulating the price of oil.

Oil price for the last 10 years from Nasdaq.com:

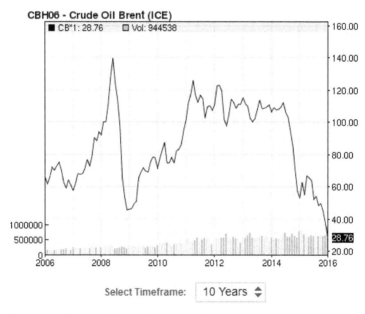

Home > Markets > Commodities > **Crude Oil Brent**

Crude Oil Brent

Latest Price & Chart for Crude Oil Brent

End of day Commodity Futures Price Quotes for Crude Oil Brent

Select Timeframe: 10 Years

Crude Oil Brent Related ETFs: BNO

My predictions

Prediction #1

For the year, it will be in $25 to $40 per barrel. Personally I do not wait for $25 as it may never materialize.

Reasons:

- Global economies have not recovered yet.
- Iran's oil will add more supply.
- OPEC and Russia cannot trim supply as their economies depend on oil export.

Prediction #2

For years later, it will return to $50 and on its way to $100.

Reasons:

- Global economies will recover (they always do). Do not know when.
- OPEC will trim supply.
- Supply will be reduced due to the current cutting down on drilling and exploration.
- Global population growth.
- Inflation (about 3% per year).
- Historical price. Recently we had oil price below $30 and then it went up to $140. Adjusted for inflation, the current price is even less than the then $30.
- As a rough estimate (depending on individual oil fields), it takes about $50 to extract, market and explore one barrel of oil (i.e. the cost of goods).

  It is better to shut down many of the oil fields such as ocean fields and oil sands at today's $30 range. OPEC cannot cut due to the payments to the loans on many on-going ventures but they should in the future.

  To supply the oil with the depressed prices is the same as spending all the money without caring about retirement.

Summary

It is a supply and demand play. It could also be a case of commodity dumping and the U.S. may try to protect its own energy industry – you hear it here first.

The Losers: OPEC. They tried to cut the price to bankrupt the shale energy ventures. You do not want to shake a baby too hard or drop a big stone on your own toe. Many lose the jobs in energy fields and railroad industry due to shipping less coal.

The Winners: Investors who buy at low price now and wait patiently for the long term. I hope we're in this role. As history shown, crisis most likely is a profit potential.

Oil and the market

Today the consumers benefit from low gas prices. Airlines benefit too if they have not hedged on fuels or are not forced to buy at fixed prices from foreign countries. However, the stocks tank with the fall of oil price, so the saving in driving for most is not worth it.

Some still argue that oil price will go to $10. If it does, I will keep on buying. As from today's $28 to $10, you lose about $18 or about 65%. However, it has the potential to go back to $120 that would be more than 400% return from $28 and 1,200% return from $10. I'm buying OIL, an ETN (similar to ETF) that is supposed to float with oil price. UWTI (3X leverage) can triple your money in either direction. I do not recommend UWTI as in one day it could wipe up their entire investment. Ignore the weekly fluctuations due to speculation by traders and look for the long term.

Usually falling oil price would benefit the market in general. However, falling too much as today is not good for the economy. Usually the market is opposite to the oil price. Today it is an exception due to the oil producing countries including the Saudis and Russia dumping foreign equities to meet their obligations. I predicted when the oil price is at $85 per barrel, then there will be less dumping of foreign equities and the high oil will affect the market (or the market will be in opposite direction of the oil price again).

China cannot build storage fast enough. They need the oil as they're blessed with polluting coal but not with oil (even oil does not generate a lot of electricity). I recommend China to buy the futures of n years at y price. This will resolve the current fluctuation and bring back the market not to correlate with the oil price.

There are many articles on the topic. Just google "Oil Price". Here is one: 1.

Update as of 2/8/2016: Barron's predicts the price will fall to $20 by April, 2016 and return to $55 by year-end of 2016. Buy OIL when it falls again and do not panic to sell. If the prediction is right, one can make over 100% in 6 months.

Update as of 5/2016: Barron's prediction is mostly wrong as oil has passed $45 per barrel. It is due to unexpected events such as the fire in Canada.

I bought OIL in Jan. 19, 2016 (one of my purchases in this period). I expected to increase in price by 50% as the oil does, but it only increased 25%. What happened to half of my profit? Consider USO as an alternative to OIL.

Expecting oil price will appreciate, it is better to bet on oil service companies instead of OIL. Here is an article on how to play the oil commodity and a site on energy ETFs. I have the annualized returns of energy ETFs and CVX from Jan. 19, 2016 to May, 12, 2016.

Symbol	Description	Ann. Return
OIL	Crude oil	33%
USO	US Oil Fund ETF	112%
OIH	Oil services	80%
XOP	SPDR Oil & Gas	138%
IYE	iShr DJ US Energy	75%
XLE	S&P Energy	76%
CVX	Chevron	81%
Average		85%
SPY		32%

http://seekingalpha.com/article/3826986-buy-oil-sell-oil-instead-put-oil-pair-trade

http://www.etf.com/channels/oil-etfs

Exploring uranium

China will have 25 or so nuclear generators on-line by 2020, 4 years away from this writing. I hope it would give this metal a boost.

With Japan's problem, uranium demand was at its historical low after inflation adjustment. We need to account for the old (more than 30 years) nuclear generators that will be decommissioned. However, the net gain is still substantial.

Source: Index Mundi

The price fell from 60 to 27 and rebounded to the current 35. The Monday quarterback would tell you to buy it at 27. Similar with oil, it is not unreasonable to double the price. The question is when. It could be 3 years or as high as 15 years.

Mining could be a different story as they need to survive from this depressed price. URA is the only ETF I can find with uranium and over 100 M. URA has many mining companies included. I will evaluate the companies in the future and at the current time frame, it is too risky for me.

Filler:

Bad management and good research
Apple and Microsoft copied a lot from Xerox's PARC including Window, mouse... without paying any royalties. Xerox should be split into two parts: bad management and good research.

VII Strategy 7 : Market correction

We have about 1 to 2 corrections every year – the frequency fluctuates. It provides a good time to enter. It is a great strategy in a side way market: Buy at dip and sell at temporary surge.

22   Correction

Market timing has been judged wrongly by many. Just check out how the two major plunges can be detected easily by my simple chart.

Corrections are harder to detect. So far, I have more rights than wrongs in detecting corrections.

Everyone has its own definition of a correction and mine is as follows. A correction is a 10% or more down from the peak of last 180 days or more than 5% down in a month. Sometimes, corrections continue to 20% loss. From my definition, there is no correction in 2013 and that is quite rare. On the average it happens at least once every year since 2000 depending on my interpretation. I also estimate two minor corrections of 5% every year if we do not have a 10% correction.

Corrections provide us opportunities to enter the market. Temporary peaks provide us opportunities to sell. They happen about one to two times a year on the average but their frequencies fluctuate widely. I usually start selling at the expected peaks, and buying at the expected bottoms. Your cash position depends on your risk tolerance. 'Buy-and-hold' investors can just ignore corrections and this chapter.

Some hints (not always reliable) predict the temporary market peak:

• Up more than 10% of the expected gain. To illustrate, you predicted this year's total return is 12% in the beginning of the year. In March, the market has already gained 12%, there is a good chance it is close to the yearly peak and you should act accordingly. Review the stocks you own and sell those with less appreciation potential first.

- The market exceeds a good percent over the last peak. Define this percent based on your risk tolerance.

- Compare the annualized market P/E (SPY or any market index ETF) to its 5-year average (10-year average is fine too).

- Foreign markets are down and ours are up by a good margin.

- The interest rate. When it rises, the market will be down.

- It happens more than three consecutive days that there are more stocks advancing than retreating.

- It happens more than three consecutive days that the number of new highs is more than the number of new lows.

- From Finviz.com, SPY's SMA200 exceeds 10% (= (Price − SMA)/SMA). SMA-200 is Single Moving Average for the last 200 sessions. It indicates it may be temporarily peaking. Use it for reference only as it is not always reliable.

- From Finviz.com, SPY's RSI(14), the relative strength index based on last 14 days, exceeds 55%. It indicates it may be overbought. For reference only as it is not always reliable.

Conclusion

Corrections are harder to detect comparing to market plunges which we have excellent results so far from 2000.

Do not bet the entire farm on corrections especially when the market is risky. Keep less than 25% of your portfolio in cash on the expected peaks.

When the market corrects, it is a buying opportunity. However, when the market starts to plunge, we should exit the market as the loss would be high. If all the conditions in the following table are exceeded, most likely the market is peaking. One's opinion.

SMA-50%	SMA-200%	SMA-350%	Avg. of the 3	RSI(14)
4%	6%	11%	9%	65%

23   Six signs of a correction

The following is an article titled "Six signs of a correction" I wrote for Seeking Alpha on June 29, 2014.

http://seekingalpha.com/article/2291605-6-signs-of-a-correction?v=1404308839

The best protection is playing defense now. The chance of a correction (10% or more) is high.

Six signs of a correction

1. All my technical indicators show the market is peaking and overbought. SPY is an ETF simulating the market of S&P 500 stocks. As of 6/29/2014, the RSI(14) is 67% and the SMA-200% is 8.35%. SMA-200% measures how far away the stock price is from its simple moving average of the last 200 trade sessions.

   You may argue that you do not believe in technical analysis. However, many institutional fund managers learn technical analysis and they will act accordingly. It is one of the many tools that hedge fund managers use to 'hedge'. Most mutual fund managers cannot practice market timing bound by the rules and regulations.

2. Newton's Law of Gravity has never been proven wrong (some humor to get your attention). What goes up must come down. The market has been up even after inflation. However, it takes a breather from time to time. A small one is called a correction and a big one is called a market plunge.
3. We did not have one such correction of 10% in 2013, so the time is ripe. The average is about one correction of 10% or more and about 1.5 corrections for 5% in a year. Many experts

predicted wrongly on a correction in 2013. I do not bet against them to be wrong two times in a row.

4. There are more articles predicting a correction than articles arguing against it. It could be a self-fulfilling prophesy. It is the herd psychology. One's opinion.

5. The market has low volumes and narrow ranges for many days may indicate that the market is changing direction. The sea is calmest before a storm.

6. I am not convinced that I can make a lot of profit even if there is no correction. To me, the market is fully valued. It is my reward / risk ratio. I prefer not to make the last buck and have a good sleep.

How to protect yourself

It depends on your risk tolerance.

1. Accumulate cash from 0% to 50%. I recommend 15% for most. 0% is for those who ignore the signs. It was a great selection for 2013. I select 50% as I'm more conservative than most.

2. Place stop orders. Adjust them when they appreciate. Some stocks are more volatile than others. I prefer to use stop orders in market plunges than corrections as corrections are too brief to be effective.

3. Short the market. I do not recommend shorting in most cases. Buying a contra ETF may help. In any case, do not gamble money you cannot afford to lose.

4. Use option to protect your portfolio.

5. Prepare a list of stocks to buy when there is a correction.

Do not treat my (or all others') predictions as gospel. Predictions are just predictions. It is like buying insurance that we do not expect to collect.

I have to admit market timing is not an exact science. Hopefully we are more rights than wrongs. However there is no guarantee "to correct or not to correct".

Summary of comments on the article

There are two camps: one who believe and one who do not believe. It is as expected. I will not take credit if there will be a correction within a month, or take the blame if there will be none in the next 3 months. From my record, I have more rights than wrongs. Here is my summary:

1. I did think of other signs as mentioned by some of my readers: interest rate, oil price, current events... I expect interest rate will start rising by the end of the year. The recent rise in oil price is due to the turmoil in the Middle East. The current events including Ukraine and the Middle East seem not to be a factor as our leader does not want to participate.

2. I do not expect a market plunge (over 30% down) as I do not see any bubbles (those bubble stocks are too few). My prediction: These bubble stocks will be half the peaks achieved in 2013 and 2014 by the end of 2014. To me, all stock trades are predictions. Some materialize and some do not.

3. Corrections are harder to detect than market plunges. After I detect a plunge, I will spend most of my time in protecting my portfolio. Most likely I'll not have time to write an article. I have full description in my books if you're interested.

Filler:

Where common sense is not common sense

Excessive printing of money is not a long-term solution. Servicing the huge debt weakens our competitiveness. The politicians just want to buy votes today and finance their campaigns. Our next generations have to pay for these huge debts.

I have never taken any business classes unless required for my engineering degrees and I can understand it via common sense. I wonder why our highly-educated (at least by their Ph.D. certificates), smartly-looking (looks could be deceiving), high salaried (many times than mine) decision makers do not understand and act on it. ###

24   Correction experiences

It seems every year we have at least one correction. Some were mild (5% down) and some were fierce (15%).

Market correction in August, 2015

I have 50% in cash before the August correction. I should have 100% if I followed my chart. However, we are just human beings blinded by our greed / fears and emotionally attached.

Stocks	Buy Price	Buy Date	Return	Sold date
AAPL	107.20	08/26/15	12%	10/19/15
GILD	105.94	08/26/15	-4%	
GM	27.69	08/26/15	12%	09/17/15
GNW	4.54	08/26/15	10%	08/27/15

Market correction in Oct., 2014

I bought the following 4 stocks from my taxable account during the first half of Oct., 2014 during the Ebola panic. It was a correction. I placed the orders from my watch list and took off on vacation. The results are:

Purchases in Oct. 2014	Return (as of 5-8-15)	Bought
AET	50%	10/15/14
STZ	42%	10/15/14
SWKS	95%	10/10/14
CI	50%	10/15/14

Market correction in June, 2013

Expecting a 10% correction, I placed buy orders on certain stocks from my watch list with 5% to 10% discount from the current prices. As of 6/2013, the market only corrected itself by about 6%. Overall, I bought 8 stocks (with LCC bought twice) and all the purchase orders were executed on 6/24/13 in my largest taxable account. Because the market did not correct by the expected 10%, not all of my buy orders had been executed.

This demonstrates how to take advantage of a correction even though it has not been predicted 100% correct. This method works most of the time but not all of the time—as the market could decline further and turn a correction into a market plunge. On the very rough average, we have two dips of about 5% (good opportunity to buy stocks) and two temporary yearly highs (good opportunity to sell stocks) each year.

After a month (7/24/13), the average return was 11% and the annualized return was 131%.

The stocks bought and their performances

Stocks	Return	Annualized Return
ALK	21%	253%
BTU	7%	82%
CF	1%	18%
CRUS	16%	191%
LCC	18%	217%
MOS	-4%	-54%
OMX	12%	148%
LCC	16%	194%
Avg.	11%	131%
SPY	7%	89%
Beat SPY	47%	47%

The average return is 11% for these 8 stocks and the annualized return is 131%. Compare it to SPY's YTD (16%) and its annualized return of 29%. The return is a little over inflated as you need to have cash available to buy stocks.

Beating the SPY for 47% indicates the good quality of the stocks in the watch list. Buy when everyone is selling.

Conclusion

In order to take advantage of the dips, prepare by:

- Accumulate cash before the dip. However, if the market keeps on rising, you may lose the extra gains for selling too early. We bet the market is at a temporary peak.

- Preparing and updating a watch list for stocks to buy. If you do not have time to maintain such a list, buy ETFs such as SPY or any market ETFs that are commission-free from your broker.

- Timing is everything. It is harder to detect corrections than market plunges especially in light of the current excessive printing of money.

Beautiful 'girl' in Thailand:

VIII Strategy 8: Calendar

There is no need to time the market from 1970 to 2000. From 2000 to 2014, the market crashed two times with an average loss of about 45%.

The apples you picked are sour but some other times are tasty from the same tree. You pick them the bad ones in the wrong time or the right ones in the right time.

Market timing is about educated guesses unless you have a time machine ☺. Hopefully we will have more rights than wrongs when we follow general guidelines. It would reduce risk and could benefit us financially in the long run.

I divide the market timing in three categories by durations as follows. All time durations are estimates.

1. Secular Cycle.   Duration: 20 years.
2. Market Cycle.   Duration: 5 years.
3. Correction.   Duration: 1 year for 10% correction.
                     Duration: ½ year for 5% correction.

25   Market timing by calendar

The following predictions are based on historical data. You may have slightly different findings depending on when you start and when you end the test.

You can load the historical data of SPY via Yahoo!Finance and check out how close or different from my predictions. They are my predictions based on historical data. Use it as a reference only.

- Presidential cycle.
  Usually the market performs worse in the first two years after the election than the next two. During the 3rd year the president has to make the economy look rosy in order to buy votes. Statistically it is the best year for the market and is followed by a good year (the election year). The government may stimulate the economy, the stock market and employment

by printing more money, lowering interest rate and lowering taxes.

Democratic presidents have better market performance statistically than Republican presidents. It is not too logical as Republicans are more pro-business traditionally.

- Olympics.
  It has been proven that the host country has a better chance that its stock market appreciates the year after. It could be due to the exposure from the Olympics and / or the huge expenses in preparing the Olympics.

The last two Olympics follow this pattern as of 12/23/2013:

Olympics Country / Year	ETF	Period	Return
United Kingdom / 2012	EWU	Jan. 3, 2013 - Dec. 23,2013	11%
China / 2008	FXI	Jan. 3, 2009 - Dec. 31, 2009	43%

Greece could be an exception. It is too small a country to host this world-class event and it has wasted too many resources by building too many white elephants that the country can never justify. Brazil depends on its export of natural resources to China, so I do not count on its Olympics effect.

Winning a lot of Olympic medals has no indication for the stock markets. Both the Russian Empire and E. German were winners but disappeared in their original forms afterwards.

- Seasonal.
  Best profitable period is: Nov. 1 to April 30 next year. It is similar to the saying 'Sell in May and Go away'. It did not work since 2009 as it was Early Recovery in the market cycle.

The market does not always happen as predicted. However, when more folks follow, it becomes a self-fulfilling prophecy. I prefer "Sell on April 15 and come back on Oct. 15" to act before the herd. The more practical strategy is to start selling in April 1 and become more aggressive (selling at closer to the market prices) when it is close to May 1. For the last five years, I do not find this prediction reliable.

The explanation of the 'summer doldrums' could be the investors cash their stocks for vacations and college tuitions in the fall. Buying quality companies at the dips could be profitable.

- The worst month: September.
  The next worst month is October. However, if there is no serious market crash during October (and this month has more than its shares of crashes), it could be the best month to buy stocks.

- The best month for the bull: November.
  However, several market bottoms occurred in October and November. The next strong month is December.

- Best 30 days: Dec. 15 to Jan. 15, next year.
  It was correct for the period of 2012-2013.

- Window dressing.
  Institution investors sell their losers and buy winners around Nov. 1. From my rough estimate and on the average, the winners have a 2% percentage point better than the market and the losers have 1% worse than the market.

  Recommend to evaluate the top 10 winners from last 10 months or YTD in Oct. 15 and sell them at 3% gain or two months later.

  Recommend to buy in Dec. and sell them 3 months later. Include the stocks with more than 30% loss for the last 11 months or YTD, sort them by Earning Yield in descending order and evaluate the top 10 stocks.

  In both cases, do not buy foreign stocks and stocks with return of capital. Ignore stocks not in the three major exchanges, with low volumes and stock prices less than $2. Do not buy in losing years such as 2007 and 2008. I have my tests with my own assumptions and I use tools not available to all.

It is a guideline only. Do not buy any stocks during market plunges. Current events should be considered first such as a potential war and the hiking of interest rate.

Afterthoughts

- I predict it will be a sideways market in the later part of 2013. I am following the sideway strategy: Buy at dips and sell at ups. One's prediction.

- Why September has a bad reputation?
  http://www.marketwatch.com/story/betting-on-septembers-terrible-odds-2013-08-27?dist=beforebell

  The September of 2013 (2 days away at the time of writing) will have more problems. Check it out how many the following are correct on Oc. 1, 2013. Use it as a future guideline to predict the next September using the current market conditions then:

  1. The market is not excessively expensive, but it is not cheap. It is due for a 5% correction.
  2. Unrest in Syria (check any unrest in your next prediction on September).
  3. High oil price due to Syria.
  4. September is a statistically bad month for the stock market. However, it could be an opportunity to invest after the correction if any.
  5. Interest rate is rising.
  6. All the above indicate the market will dip. However, the rosier outlook is the global economies are improving even slowly.

- January effect.
  The performance of January may determine how the entire year performs. I cannot find any rationale but it has been proven right statistically.

- Earnings period announced in Jan., April, July and Oct. would cause big swings in stocks when they have surprises. Earning revisions could be a good predictor.

http://www.investopedia.com/terms/e/earningsseason.asp

Links
Presidential Cycle:
http://www.investopedia.com/articles/financial-theory/08/presidential-election-cycle.asp

Calendar-based market timing:
http://stock-chartist.com/2010/10/calendar-based-market-timing/

Calendar market timing for 2013:
http://www.investorecho.com/archives/8047

26   Summary

I made the following charts so it is easier to time the market by calendar.

All dates are inclusive.

No.	Metric		Score
1	Seasonal	Nov. - April, Score = 1	
2	Best Month	Nov., Score = 1	
		Sep., Score = -1	
3	Best Days	Dec. 15 – Jan.15 Score = 1	
4	Presidential Cycle	Election Year, Score = 1	
		1st Year in Office, Score = -1	
		2nd year, Score = -1	
		3rd year, Score = 2	
5	Presidential[3]	Democratic = 1 Republican = -1	
6	Market Cycle	Early Recovery, Score = 3	
		Up, Score = 2	
		Peak, Score = 1	

7	SPY (Finviz.com)	SMA200% > 8%[2] Score = -1	
		SMA200% < 0 Score = -1	
		RSI(14) > 65% Score = -1	
		Grand Score	

Footnote.

[1]   Refer to Market Cycle chapter on how I define phases of a cycle.

[2]   For simplicity, use Finviz.com. Enter SPY and you will find SMA200% and RSI(14) to predict whether the market is peaking and overbought.

[3]   I'm political neutral. The selection is based on historical statistics.

Add up all the scores. The passing grade is 0. According to my table which is based on my personal selections/preferences, the market is favorable when the grand score is 1 or higher. I bet it is the first time you see such a scoring system for market timing.

Sectors for market cycle

Market Phase[1]	Favorable		Unfavorable
Early Recovery	Financial, Technology, Industrial		Energy, Telecom, Utilities
Up	Technology, Industrial		
Peak	Mineral, Health Care, Energy		
Bottom	Consumer Staples, Utilities		Consumer Discretionary, Technology, Industrial
Seasonal	**Favorable**		**Unfavorable**
Winter	Energy, Utilities		
End of year	QQQ, EWG		
Olympics	ETF for host country[2]		

Footnote.

[1]   Refer to Market Cycle chapter on how I define phases of a cycle.

[2]   Buy it next year after Olympics. It could be due to higher GDP or the publicity. However, be selective. Greece is too small a country to host an Olympics.

IX Strategy 9: Interest sensitive

Buy long-term bond ETFs when the interest rate is high (say > 5%) and short-term bond ETFs when the interest rate is low (say < 2%).

As of 2016, high interest stocks and ETFs lose some of its previous luster.

27 My A.B.C. on bonds

Bonds are classified into several categories and each has its different characteristics. Briefly, they are classified as 30-year Treasury bonds, 20-year Treasury bonds, 10-year Treasury bonds, short-term Treasury bonds, municipal bonds, investment-grade corporate bonds and high-yield (junk) bonds.

As of 5/2013, the long-term Treasury bonds are very risky. The interest rate is so low and it has no way to go but up. It will when the economy is improving. I do not expect we are following Japan's low interest rates for last decades.

Here are random comments on bonds.

- Japan has almost virtually zero interest rate for a long while. If you borrow 1 M from them at almost 0% and invest in another country's bond at 8%, you may think you win. However, you need to consider the risk in converting the country's currency back to Japanese Yen, inflation, bond loss, and taxes.

- In 2008, almost all assets lost. However, some high-yield bonds (or junk bonds) made over 40% in 2009. To illustrate, you bought these bonds yielding about 8% dividends in the beginning of the year. The government lowered the interest rate to stimulate the economy and hence the average yield was about 1% at the end of the year. The bonds you held yielding 8% were worth far more than the current bonds yielding 1% as they provide better dividends for years to come.

- As of 4/2012, the interest rate is almost too low to invest in bonds to me.

  Even the king of bonds made the wrong call. Do not bet against the Fed as they control the interest rate. They will raise the interest rate when they think the economy is ready.

  Conventional wisdom tells us to balance your portfolio with a combination of bonds and stocks in proportional to the risk tolerance, which for some is determined by their ages. I prefer the reward/risk ratio and only buy bonds when interest rate is expected to fall which usually occurs after the first six months of a market plunge. The government has to stimulate the economy by lowering the interest rate in almost all recessions.

  Repeating the important prediction, as of 4/2013, the long-term bond crash seems to be coming. When the economy improves, the interest rate will rise. The interest rate is so low now that it has no way to go but up. It will affect adversely to the bonds you're holding especially the ones with low interest rates and long maturity from today.

- The government bond prices could collapse when its issuing country is printing too much and depreciating its currency.

  A bond at 20% yield may not be good if the company/country has more than 25% chance to default on their bonds.

- Those holding the GM bonds before the reorganization (i.e. the first bankruptcy) lost more than 40% of the bond values. Corporate junk bonds (i.e. high yield bonds) have its risk. Buy a bond fund or ETF on corporate bonds.

- The muni bonds are risky to me. I do not really care about the small tax advantages. Many may default. If you still want to buy them, buy a bond fund to spread out the risk instead of buying individual muni bonds. Detroit bankruptcy is a good example of this. This article was published far earlier than the collapse of several towns in California and now Detroit.

- The long-term bond price moves in the opposite direction of the interest rate. It is about a 1 to 5 ratio by my rough estimate. If the interest rate moves 5% up, then the long-term bond price would moves 25% down. It is very rough estimate as it also depends on how long will the bond matures.

- Few sell the bond until it matures. If you need a steady income, buy government bonds at an acceptable rate (for example, greater than 8%). 2012 is not a good year to buy bonds with the low interest rates. Some bonds did default and the owner lost most or even the entire investment. The GM bonds before its first bankruptcy is one of them though it is quite rare.

- China has been a big buyer to our US treasury bonds. China does not want to kill the goose that lays the golden eggs. They need a good economy in the USA in order to sell their stuffs, which would create jobs for its citizens.

Afterthoughts

- This article was originally written in 2012. If you followed the advice not to buy long-term bond, you will save a lot of money. The traditional allocating between bonds and stocks is wrong. The decision of buying long-term bonds should be based on the current interest rate and its direction.

- Bond ETFs: TLT (20+years Treasury Bond).

  Contra Bond ETFs: TBF (Short of TLT). Click here for an article on contra Bond ETFs.
  http://seekingalpha.com/article/1305371-strategies-for-a-rising-rate-environment-inverse-bond-funds?v=1365862967&source=tracking_notify

  Click here for other bond and contra bond ETFs.
  http://seekingalpha.com/article/1305371-strategies-for-a-rising-rate-environment-inverse-bond-funds#comment_update_link

- To respond to my 'Edu-mercial' (my new term) in 5/29/13, JTS said, "Very educational. Thanks! I'll be out my bond funds end of the day."

- Using rising interest rate as an example, the long-term Treasury bonds with lower interest rate may not fare well than the newly-issued, long-term Treasury bonds with higher rate

- Many financial advisors are trained to sell bonds. Many split the investment into stocks and bonds according to the client's age. It makes sense to them and their clients. It does not make sense to me especially on long-term bonds which are interest sensitive.

  Bonds do not have a better record than stocks. As in my chapter on Market Cycle, I advise to buy long-term bonds only when interest rate is high and / or the rate is going to plunge. Muni bonds have been advised to stay away more than a year ago and now we have Detroit, a major city, going to bankruptcy.

- Avani: This article is mind blowing. I read it and enjoyed. I always find this type of article to learn and gather knowledge.

- Buying a bond fund and an individual bond could be quite different. Bond funds usually buy a large number of bonds maturing in different periods. The mature periods are according to the objective of the fund such as long-term bond funds.

- There is a way to structure buying funds varying in maturity periods to lower the risk of the interest rate fluctuations. Check your broker to see whether they provide such a tool.

Links
Bonds:
http://en.wikipedia.org/wiki/Bond_%28finance%29
Fidelity:
Bonds vs. Bond Funds
https://www.fidelity.com/learning-center/mutual-funds/bond-vs-bond-funds

28 Muni bonds

Unlike the Federal government, states and munis do have to balance the budget and we are getting more cities bankrupt than previously predicted. We have to bite the bullet somehow otherwise we can never service our growing debts. We're running out of suckers like China to lend us money.

If you read this article on 7/2012, you should save a lot by selling all your muni bonds and long-term bonds described in last chapter.

- States will not bankrupt, but muni bonds will lose a lot of their values. QEn will be used to rescue the state. Property and state taxes will be raised if not already been raised. A lot of foreclosures usually mean less local taxes for the local government.

- State/muni bonds together with Federal bonds will have the junk status, so in the future it is harder to raise money that is needed for any public project.

- Cut down the number of state employees.
  It is easy to cut about half of the state workers and you will not notice any loss in service (as most of them work short hours and are not motivated under the union's umbrella). I just get sick of the routine 'discoveries' on how few hours they work as reported by our newspapers while we've about 18% real unemployment / under-employment rate.

  However, the firemen, policemen, and teachers should be paid fairly and they should not be cut.

- Cut their pensions and increase retirement age requirements. Most state workers have just a little less than their regular salaries in retirement and they retire at a young age. Most big companies do not have pensions now.

- Cut the entitlements/benefits that encourage folks not to work such as the generous benefits to teenage mothers. Cut the free medical care to illegal aliens. All expenditures have to be a fair percentage of our GDP not how much we can borrow and how important for buying votes.

- We do not need large government, but lean and mean government to provide us efficient services. All those taxes are not good for the economy and businesses (how can you compete with those foreign countries with minimal taxes). Without business expanding (not government expanding), we do not have real jobs.

Afterthoughts

- We need to set up a law to require the federal government to balance the budget and not to be the world's policemen which we cannot afford.

- Our experts told us to stay away from munis. They're wrong in timing – well you do not want to fight the Fed in the short term. However, their arguments are not wrong. Muni government seldom default their bonds as they cannot issue new bonds in the future if they do.

  The reality is: Some municipals are just dying and they just cannot keep up paying the interest expenses and obligations. There are better places to invest.

29 Dividend stocks

This is a popular strategy now. We have a lot of retirees who depend on investment incomes. The low interest rates in CDs and bonds drive these folks to dividend stocks.

Here is a simple screen to find these stocks. First find the stocks that have dividend rate more than 2% (about half of S&P 500 stocks). Take out those sectors that give dividends as a return of equity (REITs and many partnerships). Eliminate the stocks with bad fundamentals such as high expected P/E, high debt (compared to companies in the same sector), etc. Next ensure they should have a good history of maintaining or increasing dividends (i.e. dividend growth).

The link is
http://www.tonyp4idea.blogspot.com/2012/06/mysteries-of-pe.html.

As of 4-2013, it has been working for the last five years if you also follow my article to skip the bank stocks, the drug companies, the miners, the insurers and small foreign companies. The stocks with good dividends fluctuate less in prices. However, when a strategy is over-used, it may not work anymore. Check the next chapter on the pitfalls.

Afterthoughts

- It makes sense not to choose the stocks with top 25 dividend yield stocks. If the yield is that good, they could have some problems. It also could be yesterday's darlings. Try the next 25 according to an article I read. Need to further analyze each stock especially on the fundamentals. Ensure the high dividend yields are not due to return of capitals as in some REITs and partnerships; it could be the reason why the top 25 dividend yield stocks do not perform.

- From Norman:
  Use CCC charts by David Fish.
  http://dripinvesting.org/tools/tools.asp

- A good article on dividend stocks.
  (http://seekingalpha.com/article/1591272-the-7-habits-of-highly-effective-dividend-growth-investors?source=kizur)

- Check their payout ratios. When the company plows back most of its profit to dividend, the company will not grow much. Many mature companies are fine in doing so. A payout ratio between 50-70% is good to me.

- Ignore the Q4 of 2012 in identifying dividend and dividend growth stocks. It is a period when companies pay extra dividends expecting higher tax rates for their stock holders next year that does not materialize.

From Norman: REITs must pay out 90% of earnings to maintain REIT status. Their dividends are taxed as ordinary income.

- Buffett on dividends.
  (http://kinderflow.blogspot.com/2013/08/dividends-warren-buffett.html)

- Buy the companies that have a lot of cash and do not pay any or much dividends. There is a good chance these companies will pay dividends or increase their dividends and the stock prices would usually appreciate. If the fundamentals do not change much, sell them afterwards.

- As of 7/2013, corporations have a lot of cash and low debt comparatively. Coupled with low interest rate and a weak economy, corporations increase dividends and buy back their own stocks.

- Buyback will not change the Supply and Demand picture of a stock. The following are all theories. When a company buys back its own stocks to reduce the number of outstanding shares, the remaining shares should appreciate in value in this aspect. However, the company uses its own cash, and hence the stock value should remain the same. It is a no-win and no-loss situation and the Supply and Demand should not affect the stock price in buyback.

  However, the management understands the value of its company and its sector it is in better than anyone. The buyback could be the best way to use the company's cash compared to giving dividends, plowing back to research / development, or taking advantage of the low interest available. They also in theory consider the total return for their average stock investor (such as tax rates...).

  In practice, most officers take care of themselves first (a human nature): How to boost the value of their stock options. In the last several years, boosting dividends has proven to be a good way to do so.

- Here are the criteria for dividend stocks.

    o Dividend yield over 2.5% (or at least .5% above the average of S&P dividend yield).
    o Dividend growth for the last 5 year is zero or higher.
    o Profit growth is positive for the last 5 years.
    o Dividend payout is under 70%.
    o P/E under 25 and earning is positive.
    o ROE is over 8%.

If you do not find too many stocks, the dividend stocks may be overbought.

DRIP

DRIP stands for dividend reinvestment plan. It uses the dividend to buy more stock of the company that pays the dividend automatically and most likely with no commission and sometimes at 2-3% discount.

I participated in these plans before. After a long while, the stocks bought from dividends worth more than the initial stocks. Need to keep track of the cost basis of the bought stocks when you sell these stocks. Check out whether the company and/or your broker offer such program. There are many sites to have more info of DRIPs such as Money Paper. Google 'DRIP'.
https://www.directinvesting.com/

---

30 Dividend stocks: potential problems

When a strategy is over-used, it creates a bubble. There is no exception except one or two with unusual circumstances (like the gold rush in 2010 due to printing too much money). When the shoe shine boy told a famous Wall Street investor he was buying stocks, the investor unloaded everything. He knew the boy did not do any research and it was the herd mentality.

When Sarah Cohen told the TV reporter she was into dividend stocks, she seems to be the shoe shine boy except she is prettier and she has a lot of skills except in investing.

When the massive money flows to ETFs specialized in dividend stocks, it is a mild bubble. History tells us the average retail investor always selects the wrong side of the market. Fidelity's money fund flow has been a good contrary indicator for the market.

Past performance does not guarantee future performance unless market conditions are the same, but it seldom happens. There are many examples abound such as the 2000's internet bust. Investing in dividend stocks is still a mild bubble by many standards. Dividend stocks perform better than the market but not by a large amount. When the financial companies such as Lehman Brothers, AIG and Bear Stern are included, dividend stocks do not perform that well.

There were several articles (at least two from WSJ) on how dividend stocks are over-valued. The premium on dividend stocks has been the highest in last 30 years compared to stocks without dividend on same fundamentals in theory.

Consider Total Return.

Total Return = Appreciation + Dividend + Covered call (if used) - Taxes − Inflation

Most likely you and I do not belong to this group who drives the market but the rich and the institution investors are. They will consider their total return. Appreciation is usually more favorable than dividend for the tax-wise rich. You can argue that all your dividends are tax-free in retirement accounts and/or your tax rate is not that high. When the account including dividends is withdrawn from the account except Roth, they will be treated as regular income under the current tax law.

You do not have to realize the gains on capital gain in taxable account. When you die, the cost basis will be stepped up. In a word, you have more control with capital gains but not with dividends. The capital gain will be proposed to be 20% (vs. about 42% max. for dividends). Check the current low-tax laws.

(http://en.wikipedia.org/wiki/Dividend_tax#United_States).

X Strategy 10: Sector subscription

31 Subscription services on sectors

When your sector portfolio is over a certain threshold (say 100,000), you may want to subscribe a sector service for your primary tool or just a second opinion.

There are many subscription services to advise us to switch between sectors, but you have to pay a fee. Most subscription services such as Zacks.com rank sectors include ranks for sectors.

The following is on sector funds (select funds in Fidelity's terms). It also indicates that Fidelity is the leader in sector funds.

In 2013 most are doing quite good beating SPY by a good margin. Here are some of them.

1. AI Stock Forecast. 39% in 2013.
2. AlphaProfit Sector Investors' Newsletter. 46%.
3. Fidelity Independent Advisor Sector Momentum. 39%.
4. Fidelity Monitor and Insight. 38%.
5. Fidelity Sector Investor. 46%.

It seems their returns are quite compatible to each other. It could be they use the same technique described in this book.

The above info is based on a MarketWatch article on sector rotation.

(http://www.marketwatch.com/story/the-top-5-fidelity-sector-strategies-of-2013-2014-01-15?link=MW_popular)

I have tried a fund that rotates sectors for you. At that time, the performance was not too good.

Additional resources

- **Fidelity Sector Fund**

Without doubt, Fidelity provides a lot of sector funds and some sector ETFs. That's why there are so many investment newsletters on their sector offerings.

From AlphaProfit, the average Fidelity Select (same as sector) fund has outperformed the S&P 500 by 4.7% annually over the last 20 years. Individual performances would be far, far better if you pick the right select funds.

I recommend picking 3 top select funds and rotating them every 3 months. There would be no need to rotate them if they are still in the top five. Sell all the owned funds if the market is plunging as detected in Chapter 4. If you rotate funds in your taxable account, be warned to pay higher taxes if they're profitable – check the current tax laws. This would be the least effort in implementing sector fund rotation using a proven newsletter such as AlphaProfit.

- Finviz.com.

It has the recent sector performance. Vector Vest selects the most timely sectors and industries. So are IBD, cnnfn.com and Zacks.

Links

There are three articles in Seeking Alpha on this topic.
Developing a Rotation Strategy Using Highly Diversified ETFs:
Part I, Part II and Part III.
http://seekingalpha.com/article/2045483-developing-a-rotation-strategy-using-highly-diversified-etfs

Sectors as of 7/2014.
http://seekingalpha.com/article/2322765-sector-rankings-for-etfs-and-mutual-funds
AlphaProfit: http://www.alphaprofit.com/
Strategy: http://etfdb.com/2013/3-sector-rotation-strategies-etf-investors-must-know/

32   Newsletters and subscriptions

Why you do not see too many reviews on investment newsletters and subscriptions in media? If it is a bad review, most likely they will not advertise in the media. If it is a good review, they may have to face legal action if the vendor's subscription or newsletter does not perform.

I've been using investment newsletters / subscriptions for years. Many are priced reasonably and some are even free. While a lot of them are garbage, some are very good.

When you have a lot of money to invest and you're not using a financial adviser and/or not subscribing to any investment service, it could be a big financial mistake. You do not want to be penny smart but pound foolish. However, you could be among the few exceptions if you have the knowledge and time to make use of the free financial data, guidance and articles from the web.

You need a computer, access to Internet and a spreadsheet in order to use most subscription services effectively.

I'm not going to compare specific systems / newsletters, but I will include general pointers on how to select them. Yesterday's garbage could be a gold mine today if the subscription improves and/or the market conditions fit what they recommend.

First, you need to find your requirements and how much time you can afford to use them. If you have $20,000 or less to invest, most likely your investment both in money and time will not pay off. Just buy an ETF and practice market timing described in this book.

Here are some pointers.

- Newsletters giving you specific stocks to buy do not require much of your time. However, if they're successful, there will be too many followers buying the same stocks to drive up the prices of the recommended stocks at least temporarily. The owner of the subscription service and his insiders will buy the recommended stocks before you. I had several of this kind of newsletter, and so far I have not renewed any one of them.

- If I found the Holy Grail in investing, do you believe I'll share it with you for $100 or so? I only will after I invest my findings first. My subscribers would push up the prices for me and then I unload them before them.

- If the volumes of the recommended stocks are small, they can be manipulated easily either by the newsletter owners and/or by your peer subscribers. The first ones to sell the recommended stocks win and the last ones to sell lose.

- I prefer systems that can find a lot of stocks by providing many searches (same as screens). However, it will take a lot of time to learn and test their performances that would require a historical database. Most likely, you need to further research on each stock screened. The screens would select a limited number of stocks for further analysis, so it will save time.

  From my experience, the best performance comes from the stocks that have been screened by more than one search especially for shorter term (less than 6 months). My theory is that they've been identified by more folks and the buyers jack up the prices. It is more profitable to buy them ahead of the herd and sell them before the herd. In any case, research the stock.

- We all receive promotional mails that they could at least triple the return of your investment. Just ignore them. If it is that good, most likely they will keep them for themselves. Same for seminars to boost some penny stocks. Most likely the recommended stocks would rise initially to lure you and other suckers to move it. Watch out!

- A 'guru' told me that he made a big fortune in silver a month ago. Guess what? He also recommended selling it two months ago and lost a lot of money in doing so. He is always right but he will not advertise the times he was wrong. We call it a double talk technique.

- There are free trial offers (or deeply discounted) for most subscription services. Take advantage of them. Some services require you to spend a lot of time, so ensure you have the time. Keep track of the performance yourself via paper trading. Do not trust their 'official' performances.

- Subscribe the newsletter to fit your style of investing. If you're a day trader, newsletters on long-term investing are not good for you. Some subscriptions handle all kinds of investing styles and you need to find the strategies and recommendations to fit your style.

- Newsletters on penny stocks are risky for most of us. They may show you a list of big winners but they do not show you their losers.

  I define penny stocks as less than $2 (officially $5) and a market cap less than 100 M. However, I do buy stocks with prices around $2 in stock price or a capital cap less than 100 M. Actually I bought ALU at $1 but ALU's market cap then was about 2 billion. The stocks with prices between $1 and $10 represent the most volatile stocks and some are real gems. They are routinely ignored by most analysts.

- There are many sectors like drugs, mines and banks that we cannot evaluate effectively ourselves. It is better to seek expert advices. Check out their past performances and take advantage of the free trial offers.

- Remember there is no free lunch in life. The higher potential return of a stock is, the riskier the stock is. To me, all trades are educated guesses. The more educated the guesses are, the higher chance they will perform in the long run.

- Some newsletters / subscriptions save us time by summarizing the financial data like a value rank and a growth rank. When the market favors growth, you use the growth rank (vs. a value rank), and vice versa.

- Be careful on the commercials particularly from radio in selling to peoples' fears and their greed by overstating without necessarily telling the whole story. There is no free lunch. It is not possible to make 30% in covered calls consistently or making another gold rush from $400 to $1,800.

- TV financial shows usually exaggerate in order to sell their staffs. Analyze before you act on the news.

- As a retail investor, most of us cannot afford to do extensive researches. Many researches and market opinions are available in the internet free. Start to search for such information from your broker's site.

- Do not trust the performances of the newsletter providers. There are many ways to manipulate their performances.

- Most compare their performances with S&P 500. It is legal for investment newsletters to inflate their performance with dividends while comparing to an index without including dividends.

  To illustrate, for the last 10 years, S&P 500 has an average annual return of 1% on appreciation and 1.5% on dividends for a total return of 2.5%. Hence, the performance of a newsletter should compare itself to 2.5% not 1%.

- The performance of last 10 years is more important than that of 25 years. Their method of stock evaluation / ranking hopefully has been improved. In addition, the last 10 years is a better prediction of the newsletter than the last 25 years as the weatherman finds out.

  More than one time, I found a popular subscription did not beat the S&P in the last 5 years but it did in the last 20 years. It could be that too many folks are using the same strategy.

- When the new major researcher takes over the subscription, s/he may not have the same expertise as the previous researcher.

- Ensure they change their strategies according to the current market conditions. For example, 5 years ago ADRs (U.S. listed stocks of foreign countries) perform far better than today.

- Few if any use real money for their portfolios, as they cannot cheat with real money. That's why you never achieve the compatible performance by following what the portfolio trades. Do not trust any performance claims even from reputable monitor services unless the portfolios are in real money or they can be verified.

  Some sample portfolios trade excessively and they may not fit your investment strategy not to mention the broker commissions and tax bites.

- When a subscription service has several strategies (say 10 for illustration), it will advertise the best returns of its top strategies (say 2 in our example) for a specific time period. The worst loser strategy will never be mentioned.

Contrary to not recommending investment services, here are very low priced or even free subscription services. By opening a small account with a broker, you can access their research. Check your current broker's website on evaluating stocks. AAII is a low-priced subscription with on-line stock research. Yahoo!Finance is very popular among investors. Seeking Alpha is a good web site. However, watch out their agenda such as selling you a product and lure you to buy recommended stocks.

Afterthoughts

- My friend told me he saw an ad that would show him how to make $500 a day for working a few minutes before the market opens. He is nice enough to share his 'discovery' with me to make me rich. If it is for real, I would be the first one to sign up. If it really works, it will not work very soon. When a strategy is over-used, it will not work. Unfortunately, a fool is born every minute as the same ad has been there for a long time.

- Currently I spend about $1,500 for all subscription services. I believe $200-$600 should cover the basic. To start, you can use your broker's web site for tools. Some have a lot of research for evaluating stocks and some even include searches. Try the biggest broker's research as they spend more on this area. Even if you do not trade with them, use their research by opening an account with the minimum balance.

- If the offer is too good to be true (like making $500 every day with little effort and little investing money), it probably is not. If they give you a free 50" TV for spending $299, most likely it is a trap with bait. Again, remember there is no free lunch.

  However, some baits are good like the free 30-day trial offer for an investment service or the free dinners I attended seminars on estate planning. It is part of the business cost. If I do not attend more than two dinners, eventually I would end up paying two free dinners for someone I do not even know. This book could be the best deal for your entire investment life if you invest time to read it, digest it and use the ideas that are applicable to you and the current market.

- One advertises the technique of using covered calls achieving 48% a year. I have seen these 'techniques' many times before such as "Making big money in the first 15 minutes before the opening bell". First I have strong doubt on the claim – it would drive all mutual funds out-of-business. Even if it were true, it will be over-used and will not be effective. Do not waste your time and money unless you believe in fairy tales.

- Do not trust their claims and the past performance may not have anything to do with the current or future performance unless they are from reliable sources.

  To illustrate how to monitor their recent performance, if they give you 20 stocks every week, save the prices and check their performance in the same period you usually hold the stocks. It has busted many well-advertised and very popular subscription services. I prefer to compare the performance to S&P 500 index. It is better to compare it both in an up market and a down market as some strategies amplify their performance by selecting riskier stocks.

- On 5/2013, I received an ad boasting how great its portfolio performs from a well-known paper on investing. The cumulative return from 2001 to today is an impressive 308% beating the S&P 500's 43%. However, if you analyze it, most of the big gains are made before 2009.

To prove it, I used their data and input their returns from 2009 to today. Their accumulative return is 37% while the S&P 500 is 66%. The more current data has better predicative power than the older data.

The moral of the story:

1. Read any claim with skepticism. Test it yourself.
2. The recent performance has better predictive power than the older data.
3. When a strategy is over-used, it will become less effective.
4. The market conditions change from time to time. Some strategies work better than others in different conditions and different phases of the market cycle.
5. Most likely their return includes dividends while the S&P 500 index does not.

Filler

How celebrities and/or newsletter owners make money for themselves

To illustrate, a TV or talk host and his staffs know what stocks they want to promote in the next show. They may have bought these stocks before the show – is it legal? The viewers or listeners follow the recommendations to move the prices up. In two or three months later, these insiders dump the stocks and the stock prices come down.

XI Strategy 11: Top-down

Basically you pick the best sector and buy the best stocks within the sector. It is the more time-consuming task and the rest of the book is devoted to this strategy.

33 Top-down investing

The nutshell is described here. Only buy stocks when the market is favorable. Find the best industry (a subsector) and then find the best stock(s) within the selected industry. In doing so, our chance of successful investing is substantially increased.

It is so simple and it has been proven by many including myself. I just wonder why it has not been extensively practiced. I offer a simple example as follows:

1. Do not invest when the market is plunging. I have a simple way to detect market plunges without any expensive subscriptions or tools.

2. Select the best industry (most are represented by an ETF or ETFs specific for the industry or sector). For example, Technology is a sector. Computer and Software are industries (subsector under Technology). From time to time I use sectors for simplicity and most free sites do not sub divide the sectors into industries. Check out the best-performed industry or sector from last month in many sites including SeekingAlpha and CNNfn.

    If you're a value investor, you may not want to choose the timeliest sector but the most under-valued sector. Value investors should hold the sectors/stocks longer (such as 6 months or even longer) for the market to recognize their values.

    In addition, you need to detect the sector/stock rotation by the institution investors who control over 75% of all trades (i.e.

smart money). They will rotate sector/stock when they find better profit potential in another sector/stock. Use stops to prevent further losses.

If you do not have time to research on stocks, trade ETFs for sectors and skip the next step.

3. The final step is to select the best stock(s) within the sector via fundamental analysis (including intangible analysis), insider trading analysis, institution trading analysis and technical analysis.

   Do not let these terms scare you. We will start with the simplest approach without any subscription and a lot of effort.

4. The next step is when to reevaluate and sell the stocks when conditions change or they meet your objectives. If the market is plunging, sell all stocks.

Stick and repeat the entire process.

The easiest retirement planning system

Have a budget and live within your means. Buy good stuffs that last for a long time. After saving enough cash for emergency and planned expenses such as vacation, new car, college, etc., invest your extra money in a retirement account (Roth IRA if allowable) with 80% in a market ETF and 20% in a short-term bond ETF.

Run the chart described in the market cycle chapters once a month. If the chart tells you to exit the market, move all to cash. Reenter the market when the chart tells you so. It beats most if not all of your financial plans from the best experts money can buy.

Using Finviz.com as a screener example

The following is an example. Fine tune the selection criteria according to your personal criteria and risk tolerance.

- Bring up Finviz.com from your browser. Select Screener, the third tab. As of 3/24/2015, we have 7066 stocks.

- For illustration, we would like to find stocks with double bottoms, a positive technical indicator. If not using the All tab, select the Technical tab. Select Pattern and then Double Bottom. Now we have 257 stocks.

- Select the Fundamental tab (next to the Technical tab). Select Forward P/E and then select "under 20". Now, we have 86 stocks.

- Select Debt/Equity less than .5. Now, we have 45 stocks. Some industries are traditionally high in debts, so you can use 'less than 1'.

- Select EPS growth Q-to-Q over 10%. Now, we have 19 stocks.

- Select the Description tab. Select Country to USA. Now, we have 17 stocks.

- Select Price > 1. Select Avg. Volume "Over 100K". Select Float Short "Under 10%. Select Analyst Recs. "Buy or better". Now we have 9 stocks.

   Now we can evaluate them one by one using Fundamental Analysis, Intangible Analysis, Qualitative Analysis and Technical Analysis. The purpose of screening is to filter the 7000 stocks to a small number (9 stocks in this case).

Skip the stocks that have the Earnings Date within 2 weeks. If you already have too many stocks in the same industry, skip that stock. You can save the screen when you register with Finviz.com. It is free. Check the performance in 3 months or so.

Modify the screen with the Pattern changed from "Double Bottom" to "Head and Shoulder" and run the screen to demonstrate how we use different technical patterns for about the same parameters. The following table summarizes our common parameters.

	Descriptions	Fundamentals	Technical
1	Country = USA	Forward P/E <20	Pattern= Double Down
2	Float Short < 10%	Earning Growth Q-Q > 10%	
3	Analyst Rec. Buy or better	Debt / Equity < .5	
4	Avg. Vol. > 100K		
5	Price > $1		

This is a sample. Use it as a frame work to other screens. Here are my explanations on the selected metrics.

Description

- Most should stick with the three major exchanges. Indexes would limit you to blue chip stocks.

- From my top down investing, your stock appreciation is determined by the market, the sector and then the stock.

  It gives you 8 sectors to select. Check out the best performance (I prefer 3 months) from the Group from the Home bar. Industry gives you the industries within the sector.

- You can trade foreign stocks. I do not trust most financial statements of foreign stocks, esp. the smaller ones. For the last few years (as of 2015), the US stock market has better performance than most foreign companies.

- Market Cap. I prefer "Small or Larger than Small". "Micro" gives you the best performance but it comes with more risk. If the micro stock is listed in one of the three major exchanges and has a daily average volume of more than 100,000 at a price over $1, it is less risky than otherwise.

Fundamentals

- I prefer Forward P/E over P/E. Need to take out stocks with Earning (E) < 0.

  PEG measures the growth of P/E. A stock with higher P/E but better growth in P/E may be a better candidate than one with lower P/E and negative growth.

- P/S is a proven metric. However, consider the type of business. P/S should be good for a retailer compared to a high tech company which does not depend on the sales volume.

- Price/Cash. Together with Debt/Equity, Pow P/E is better than P/E. If a company has cash of $10 per share and the stock price is $5, most likely the stock is underpriced unless some lawsuits and other problems are surfacing.

- P/B is the grand daddy's metric together with P/E. Mature companies may not include some important assets in the book and/or a promising new product(s).

- To me profit growth for this quarter compared to the quarter prior year is important. It takes care of seasonal fluctuations. Sales growth of 100% with decreasing profit is not a good sign as indicated in the internet era.

- ROE measures the performance of the management.

- Debt/Equity. I prefer it less than 50% (or .5). However, many industries such as utilities borrow heavily.

- Payout ratio and dividend yield are primary metrics for dividend seekers.

34   Fundamental metrics

Unfortunately there are very few fundamental metrics for sectors. The following are common metrics for stocks in case you want to trade stocks within a sector. The following info is available from the selected web site. However, you can average the top 10 or so stocks in the sector ETF for that sector.

Yahoo!Finance:
- P/E (based on last twelve months as ttm).
- Avg. volume (do not buy ETFs that are thinly traded).
- Yield (ttm).
- Net Asset (do not buy ETFs whose assets are low).
- YTD return (check the date it is based on).

Introduction

The simple formula to make money is finding value stocks and waiting for the market to realize their values. Only buy when the market is not risky. Most successful investors are doing this.

Basic metrics

The book value of a stock is simply the net worth of a company (= Assets − Liabilities). When the stock price is higher than the book value per share (i.e. 'Stock Price / Book Price' > 1), it is over-valued. When this ratio is more than 2 or less than 0.5, you have to be cautious and find the reason. Many intangible assets such as the competitive edge have not been priced into the book value. Hence a high ratio may not be an alarm. When it is way underpriced, there may be a critical reason.

Intrinsic Value includes the intangibles such as patents. However, both the Book Value and Intrinsic Value have not been convincing as predictors to me from my tests and experiences. Briefly, describe some basic but important metrics here.

- Expected Earning Yield (E/P). The future appreciation depends on future earnings and the current price of the stock (you do not want to overpay). I prefer a range between 5% and 30%.

- Growth of Earnings and growth of sales. Compare them to their rates in the same quarter last year. I prefer 10% or higher.
- The management is measured by ROE. I prefer 10% or higher.
- How safe it the company? It is measured by 'Debt/Equity'. I prefer less than .5 (same as 50%). However, some industries are debt intensive.

These are the ratios readily available from many sites including Finviz.com except reversing the expected P/E for expected Earning Yield. There is no need to dig into the complicated financial statements to start. Just ensure the metrics are up-to-date.

The predictability of most metrics changes according to the current market conditions. Monitor their performance and act accordingly. I prefer E/P but Earnings/Sales had better predictability in my 7/2015 test.

Market Cap (Capitalization)

Market Cap = Total no. of outstanding shares * share price

For beginners, I recommend to buy U.S. stocks with market cap greater than 800 M (million). Here are the current conventions (everyone's convention is different) and they should be adjusted to inflation.

Class	Market Cap (million)
Nano Cap	< $50M
Micro Cap	$50M to $250M
Small Cap	$250M to $1B (billion)
Mid Cap	$1B to $10B
Large Cap (Blue Chip)	$10B to $50B
Mega Cap	>50B

The higher the cap is, the less risky is the stock. Nano Cap and Micro Cap are reserved for speculators or owners of the companies. Small Cap and Mid Cap are for knowledgeable investors as most institutional investors would skip the stocks in these caps especially Small Cap. Large Cap, Mega Cap and some Mid Cap are the stocks traded by institutional investors. They are thoroughly researched continuously.

ROE
Return of equity (ROE) could be the most important financial indicator to determine how well the management is doing the job. However, in recent years, this metric has been over-used and it loses its reliability in prediction.

The company's return on equity for at least the last five years would indicate how the stock price endures major financial downturns as well as upturns.

Comparing the ROE to the average ROE for the sector is a good indicator on how well the company is managed compared to its peers. Some sectors including utilities have low average ROEs.

My metrics

My current favorites are Expected P/E, PEG, Analysts' Opinions, Short % of outstanding shares, Free Cash Flow, ROE and Debt Load / Equity.

In addition, I use many summarized metrics from different sources. For example, one of my subscription services gives me a composite rank for fundamentals and another one for momentum. To illustrate, click here for Blue Chip Growth which is free currently for stock analysis. Enter IBM as the stock symbol. As of 2/2013, it gives C for a Total Grade, D for Quantity Grade and B for Fundamental Grade. The Total Grade is usually a composite grade of other grades.

Use the metrics to screen through the stocks to reduce the number of stocks for further consideration. After being burnt several times by small Chinese companies, I just skip most of them.

Mid, high and low values of common metrics

Metric	Mid Range	Low Range	High Range
P/E (last 12 months)	< 10	>40	< 4
Price / Cash Flow	< 12	>30	< 4

Price / Sales	< 2.5	>3	< .2
Price / Book	< 2.0	>4	< .2
PEG	< 1.5	>2	< .2

High Range means good values (although in this table it means low numbers), but sometimes it is too good to be true. Low Range means bad values. To illustrate, many internet stocks in 2000 had P/E over 40 (bad) while a neglected bargain stock has a P/E of 3 (supposed to be good). A bargain could also mean there could have some hidden problem. In reality, I prefer the Mid Range. Using P/E to illustrate, it should be between 4 and 10. Adjust the range according to your personal tolerance and the current market conditions. If the market trend is up, you may want to relax the range to 5 to 12 for example otherwise you cannot find too many stocks for further evaluation.

These values are my selections based on data for about 10 years. They are used for prediction the performance of a stock in a year; check the ranges every 6 months in the current market.

The metrics with high-range and mid-range values offer better prediction for stock price appreciation. From the above table, the stocks with low-range values have a better chance than other stocks to lose money in a year or so. Some favorable numbers could be high values instead of low values such as ROE.

However, the range values could change. When the market favors momentum or you do not keep stocks for less than a month or so, the momentum metrics including PEG and price growth could be better predicators. We need to check whether the current market favors which group of the metrics: Value or Growth – some web sites and subscription services identify the current favorite. In addition, the performance of each metric should be evaluated every 3 to 6 months. In addition, new range values need to be adjusted to in the above table.

Fundamental metrics take a longer time (about 6-12 months vs. 1 month for momentum metrics) for the performance to materialize. The metrics in the above table beside PEG are all fundamental metrics.

Example of searching with high range values

Stocks with low-range values for most metrics (such as 40 in P/E in the above table) could be risky. Hence, select the stocks with the mid-range value (e.g. 10 for P/E). Avoid the low-range values indicated by the metrics.

Here is one example of selecting stocks with high range values of P/E and P/B. Most likely, you cannot find too many stocks with these criteria.

$$E > 0 \quad \text{and}$$
$$P/E < 4 \text{ and}$$
$$P/B < .2$$

E is earning per share and we need the company to be profitable.

High range values could indicate something wrong with the company, e.g. a lawsuit pending. I would consider a P/E of less than 4 is suspicious. However, very small companies are often neglected by the market, so they could be solid companies. Don't forget to do your due diligence and spend more time in thoroughly evaluating the stock and its industry.

The stocks with low-range values have a greater chance to lose money in the next year or so. That is proven statistically as a group despite some exceptions. AMZN[2] is not a valued stock by its high P/E or its high P/B. However, if the company is investing for the future by building infrastructure and capturing market share, you may ignore these unfavorable metrics. Personally I prefer fundamentally sound companies today.

Note. P/B is not a good metric for established companies and / or companies with a lot of research such as IBM. Many metric formulae are outdated due to ignoring intellectual properties, patents and market appeals such as brand names.

Example of a search for mid-range values
$$E > 0 \text{ and}$$
$$P/E < 10 \text{ and}$$

P/E > 4

In this case, you only include companies with positive earnings and P/Es within the range from 4 to 10 exclusively. You should find many companies with the mid-range values of P/Es.

Add other filters such as minimum price, market cap and average volume. If you do not find too many stocks, relax your criteria (start with mid-range values in the table), and vice versa to limit the number of stocks. If you find stocks usually with a screen but not today, it usually means that the market is over-valued that you cannot find many bargain stocks.

Again, it is the first step to narrow down the number of stocks to be analyzed. Your metrics will not cover stocks with special situations. For example, IBM always has a high Price/Book value as long as I can remember and it does not mean it should be excluded.

The searches based on fundamental metrics help us to narrow stocks for further evaluations. Occasionally I abandon the scoring system for some stocks under special conditions.

Compare company's metrics to its sector averages[1]

This could be the most powerful comparison: Compare Apples to Apples.

You may want to compare the metrics of a company to the averages of that sector. The average of supermarket's P/S is extremely low and hence it has no meaning to compare a supermarket's P/S to most other sectors. Some sectors like utilities need high debt to run a utility company.

However, when the average P/E or other metric of a sector is suddenly lower than its historical average, it could mean that sector is out-of-favor and/or the sector is having better value.

This following table compares Apple to its sector and a retail sector on a specific date for illustration. All the metrics will change.

Metric	Apple	Computer	Retail
P/E	11	19	24
(5 year average)	16	17	15
PEG	.6	N/A	1.4
Price /Cash Flow	9.4	8.1	9.2
Price /Book	3.3	3.0	3.6
EPS Growth	-6%	-42%	2.6%
(last 5 years)	62%	45%	11%
Operating Margin	20%	15%	8%
ROE	30%	14%	19%
Debt / Equity	2%	7%	88%
Inventory Turnover	76%	53%	4.55x

From the above table, some metrics only make sense for an industrial sector (Computer for Apple). In this case, you want to compare AAPL to Computer, and not to Retail.

Debt / Equity indicates that the retail sector needs to borrow more than computer sector for example. So is Inventory Turnover.

Top down approach

First, compare whether the market is risky. Second, select the best sector; there are many sites including finviz.com to select the best sector. Then compare the fundamental metrics of the major stocks within that sector.

Some metrics do not apply

Using financial institutions as an example, usually P/B is more useful than P/CF. However, the quality of loan (not a metric here) is more important than all metrics as we found out in 2007. P/S is more important for retails. However, the expected P/E is most important for most other sectors.

When you believe a sector is best currently, select stocks only for this sector, a criterion available in many screeners.

Compare metrics to its five-year average

If the company's five-year average of P/E is 20 and today it is 10. It is 100% under-valued by this standard. Try other metrics such as debt/equity.

Growth Metrics

The growth metrics are growth rates of the stock price, sales, earnings, etc. They are useful for growth investors.

Even for value investors, earning growth rate is very important, as most stocks with substantial gains have increased their earnings growth first. If the earning has grown but the price remains the same (i.e. PEG), then the potential for price appreciation will be higher and most likely it will return to the historical average P/E.

Momentum Metrics

Momentum metrics is part of growth. The rates of increase of the stock price, the volume... are the major metrics. Earnings revision is another one especially in earning announcement seasons (4 times a year). Many subscription services provide a composite rank with name Timely or similar name. In my momentum portfolio, I use these metrics and ignore all other metrics as my average holding period is less than 30 days for momentum strategy.

Insiders' buying
Insiders sell their stocks for many reasons. When insiders buy a lot of their companies' stocks at market prices, take notice. Insiders know better than anyone about the health of their companies and their industries.

Select Insiders' purchases from one of the available sites such as Finviz.com. Ignore the option exercises. I prefer the high ratios of Net Total Purchase Value / Market Cap and the purchases by more than one insider. Be careful that the insider did not purchase the stocks after selling similar amount of stock.

OpenInsider is a good site for this info.

InsiderSights is a good one too with more capable tools that would take more time to learn.

Where to get the metrics

You can get this information from the web site with no or low cost such as finviz.com, your broker's site, AAII (very low cost) and Blue Chip Growth (free so far).

The following subscriptions are at a little higher cost but they are still less than $1,000 per year: Value Line, IBD, Zacks, Vector Vest and Stock Screen 123. Many data from different vendors are duplicated. You will save time by concentrating on one or two sources.

Many vendors provide a composite metric such as a value metric to cover P/E, debt... and a timing metric to cover Technical Analysis indicators, PEG, price appreciation rate...

Short % is a useful metric available in finviz.com. For Fidelity customers, you can click on Research and then Stock. Enter the stock name, and then click on Detailed. I find Fidelity's Analysts' Opinions quite useful.

Finviz.com provides a lot of good information free of charge. It also provides a screen function.

Other sources are: Insider Cow, NASDAQ Guru Analysis ...

Monitor the recent performance of the metrics
The predictability of most metrics has proven not to perform consistently as many investors and fund managers found it out. My theory is that the specific metric works better in some market conditions than others. To test which ones work better currently, check their performance in the last three months and use those that perform well. This is my scoring system in the book Scoring Stocks is based on.

Why some metrics fail sometimes
Most investors are using metrics to screen stocks, but few are successful consistently. Some investment companies have top

analysts dedicated to projects looking for the right strategy. My guess why they fail:

1. Metrics need to be monitored to see its effectiveness on current market conditions.

2. Besides fundamental metrics, there are many intangibles.

3. When they have too many followers on the same metrics, they will not work such as ROE in last several years.

4. Fundamentals need time (at least 6 months) to reflect the value of the stock. You're swimming against the tide as a fundamentalist. Trading momentum stocks using basic fundamentals will not work.

5. Watch out 'Garbage in and garbage out'. Some emerging countries do not have organization similar to SEC to ensure the integrity of the financial statements of a company and some audit firms are being paid to cover their eyes. Even there are frauds in some U.S. companies and their auditors.

6. The metrics are derived from obsolete financial statements. Check out the date. The most updated one could be available from the company's website.

7. Some companies borrow a lot of money to dress up the metrics such as P/E and ROE. They will look good short-term but not long-term. Ensure the debt/equity has not been increased recently for this purpose. I recall one utility spin-off has incredible fundamentals except the debt load. It is so high that all these fundamentals will deteriorate in the future due to servicing its high debts.

Footnote

[1] The stocks are classified into sector and then sub classified into industries. For example, oil is a sector and oil exploration and oil services are industries under the oil sector. For simplicity, I intermix the terms here as many sectors do not need further sub classifications for this discussion.

[2] AMZN is not a value stock by any standard. As of 1/1/2013, its P/E (from last 12 months) is 157 and P/B is 15. Both fall far into my low-range values. Its price rises from 256 from 1/1/13 to 270 today (1/22/13). Today its P/E is ridiculously over 3,000. The investors are betting AMZN's internet sales will take over the concrete stores and its investors do not care about profit but for market share. Does it sound like familiar in the internet era? Its price momentum is indicated positively by any chart. It may be a good stock for traders, but it is too risky for a swing trader and a long-term investor like me (yes, I wear two hats). I do not short stocks in a rising market, but this could be an exception.

Afterthoughts

- Click here to check how others use metric to evaluate the fundamentals of a company.
  http://ebmyth.blogspot.com/2012/12/afterthoughts-metrics-for-stock.html

- The only recommendation from a very popular investment book to select stocks is the return of equity (ROE). I will save you the time and money to read that book. I read the entire book in an hour at Barnes and Noble's and it saved me some money / time, not to mention cutting down trees for that book. Basically it does not work today.

- DAL has an interesting Debt / Equity of over -1000% due to the negative equity. For a comparison, you may want to use Debt / ABS(Equity).

- Once in a while, I found the financial data are not consistent from different sources. Try to check out any discrepancy in the dates of the financial data of the sources. The financial statements from the company websites usually have the most updated data.

- Current Ratio = Current Asset / Current Liability. If it is below 1, then the company is having a tough time to meeting its current cash obligation.

- Dividend Yield is a valid metric for matured companies. I do not use it to evaluate growth companies or companies that need to plow back cash for research and development.

- If you use finviz.com, you find three margins: profit, gross and operating. I prefer to use profit margin that is more useful to compare companies in different sectors.

  http://www.investopedia.com/terms/p/profitmargin.asp
  http://www.investopedia.com/terms/g/grossmargin.asp
  http://www.investopedia.com/terms/o/operatingmargin.asp

  Use Wikipedia for more description.

- Enron had millions in profits but negative cash flows. Earnings can be manipulated but not the cash flows.

  Insiders' selling usually does not cause any alarm unless excessively. Most insiders sell most of the stocks they have before these companies bankrupt. Just common sense!

- Why fundamentals are important.
  (http://seekingalpha.com/article/1612442-its-shorting-season)

  On the same day when this article was published, RVLT was up 10% due to increasing sales on the earnings conference. However, the company is still not profitable. It shows how tough is shorting even with good arguments.

- Due to my ignorance, limited time or my short period of holding stocks, I have not used intrinsic value that often.

  Book value is different from intrinsic value. Book value is calculated by summing up the values of all pieces of a company such as a building and a machine.

  Intrinsic value is the real value of a company. When two companies have the same book value and market cap, the company that generates more profit than the other one usually has higher intrinsic value. When the intrinsic value is higher than the stock price, it is underpriced in theory.

There are many articles in Seeking Alpha on this topic.
http://en.wikipedia.org/wiki/Intrinsic_value_%28finance%29

- Why CF was very cheap? Jacob could find the reason as he wrote as an example for Intangible analysis:

  It is always a good idea to try to understand why something is cheap. How do you know the other side is wrong when you don't even know what their view is? CF has been pretty cheap for a long time, though now seems particularly cheap.

  It is not an exact comparable to the other industry players as its profits come mainly from Nitrogen, which requires no natural resources other than air and energy to produce. POT, MOS, IPI and to some extent AGU have more phosphate and potash exposure, which require mineral reserves. In other words, CF is a commodity chemical producer and the others are miners. And AGU is as much a distributor and retailer as a producer.

  Investors are concerned about the large amount of nitrogen capacity slated to come on stream in the US over the next several years. What I believe the negative case is missing are:

  - Not all announced projects get built, for various reasons.
  - Projects usually take longer than projected.
  - CF still has a few years of excellent FCF before this new capacity starts, so it can buy back most of its shares if it wants, over 3-4 years.
  - Even if all the projects get built, the US will still be a net importer, so Nitrogen will still price off the world price.

Links
Expected P/E:
http://www.tonyp4idea.blogspot.com/2012/06/mysteries-of-pe.html

PEG: http://en.wikipedia.org/wiki/PEG_ratio
Short %:

http://www.investopedia.com/university/shortselling/shortselling1.asp#axzz2LNDvpemo

Blue Chip Growth:
http://navelliergrowth.investorplace.com/bluechip/password/index.php?plocation=%2Fbluechip%2F

Openinsider:	http://www.openinsider.com/
finviz:	http://finviz.com/
terms:	http://www.finviz.com/help/screener.ashx
Insider Cow:	http://www.insidercow.com/
Current Ratio:	http://en.wikipedia.org/wiki/Current_ratio

How to find quality stocks.
http://seekingalpha.com/article/2381395-how-to-identify-quality-stocks-and-is-there-really-alpha-to-be-had

Finviz parameters

Most metrics are described in Finviz (via Help), Investopedia and/or Wikipedia and the chapter on P/E. The following are my personal comments and why some metrics are more important than others. Compare the ratios to the companies in the same sector and also its averages from the last 5 years.

Also, they are roughly based on the flow of Finviz skipping those metric I believe not too important. You can also place your cursor on the metric to have the description from Finviz. Some metrics are left blank when they are zero or negative.

- **Index**. Usually we use Exchange. Most of us trade stocks in the three major exchanges in the USA. Stocks listed over-the-counter are too risky to many. Skip the stocks in local exchanges and foreign exchanges if you are not an expert on these stocks.

- **Market Cap** (MC). To me, stocks below 50M are risky even they could be very profitable. Ensure the Avg. Volume is at least 10,000 shares or your order is less 1% of the average volume. Some small stocks are controlled by the owners with small volumes. In this case you cannot sell your stock easily.

Float = Outstanding shares – Insider shares.

Usually it does not matter as they are typically the same. However, it does for small companies with large insider shares. Most of these owners do not want to sell their family businesses and hence they reduce the chance of being acquired entirely or partly for good prices.

- If **Expected P/E** is not provided, use the P/E which is based on the last 12 months. Alternatively, calculate the E by using the E from P/E and multiplying it by its growth rate. It may not be seasonally adjusted. I prefer Expected P/E (or called Forward P/E) as it has better predictability power from my limited research.

- **Cash / share**. It is used to calculate Pow P/E and Pow EY. To illustrate, if the stock is $10 and it has $10 cash / share without debt (i.e. Debt/Equity = 0), most likely it is underpriced as you can get the whole company for nothing. You should find out why the price is so low.

- **Dividend %** is useful for income investors. The payout ratio should not be more than 30% except for matured companies.

- **Recs**. Select stocks with 1 or 2. Do not base on their recommendation alone. There have been many bad recommendations that would cost you a fortune.

  If your broker is Fidelity, use their Analysts' Opinion. It is based on the previous performances of the analysts. Just for this feature alone, I recommend opening an account with minimum requirements – I do not get any compensation from them. Also, it would spare you from reading 30 or so pages on this topic that I believe it is a waste of time.

- **PEG** is a measure of the growth of P/E and hence a growth metric. The lower, the better. If there are two companies with the same P/E, the one with better PEG is better. EPS Growth is similar metric with Earnings. I prefer PEG over EPS growth. If two companies have the same E/P, the Earnings Growth (EPS Q/Q) would be the tie breaker.

- **P/B**. Book value (= Total Assets − Total Liabilities) may not include intangible asset such as patents. Do not trust it 100%, so is ROE which is based on book value. Negative equity is possible when Total Liabilities is more than Total Assets.

- **P/FCF**. I prefer it greater than 0 and less than 50 for value investors.

- **Sales Q/Q** reduces the seasonal deviation. To illustrate, retail sales for Christmas season should compare it to same season in prior year.

- **EPS Q/Q**. Same as above. I prefer the growth of EPS over Sales. The Q/Q ratios are growth metrics. When a company terminates its unprofitable product(s), its Sales Q/Q could be down but its EPS Q/Q could be up. In 2000, many internet companies had great Sales Q/Qs but negative EPS Q/Qs.

  When the company buys its own shares, EPS could be misleading as E is fixed and the number of shares is reduced.

- **Profit Margin**. I prefer it over Gross Margin and Oper. Margin which does not include interest expenses and taxes. When you sell software, the Gross Margin is high as it does not include development, support and marketing, etc. A retail store has low Gross Margin.

- **Short Float**. I prefer it less than 10%. If it is greater than 10%, the shorters could find something wrong with the company. If it is over 25%, I would check the fundamentals. If they are good, I buy it betting on a short squeeze. It has been risky but proven to be profitable to me.

- Technical metrics: **SMA-20**, SMA-50 and SMA-200. If they are all positive, it means the trend is good. SMA-20 is short-term trend and SMA-200 is long-term trend. If you are short-term swing investor, stick with short-term trend and vice versa.

- **RSI(14)**. If it greater than 60% (some use 65%), it is overbought. If it is under 30% (some use 25%), it is under bought. Use it as a reference. Most stocks making new heights are always overbought.

- Management performance is measured by ROA. It is also judged by Analysts' Rec. and Inst Own (except for small companies). The confidence of their own ability, the company and its sector is measured by Insider Own and Insider Purchase.

- Avoid all bankrupting companies at all cost. Debt/Equity, P/FCF, Cash/Sh., P/B, Profit Margin, Forward P/E, Short Float, RSI(14), SMA20% and SMA50 would give us hints. Need to summarize all the info and study many other factors such as obsoleting products (including drugs).

More useful information:

- The price chart. It has a lot of features such as the resistance line. Some charts include technical indicators such as double top (a bearish warning) and double bottom (a bullish sign).
- Description under the symbol. It briefly describes what the company (sector and industry) does and its country of registration. You want to buy a stock in a sector in its uptrend. Industry is a sub sector. For example according to Finviz, Apple is in Consumer Goods sector and Electronic Equipment industry. If you do not want to buy foreign stocks, skip it if it is not listed in the US exchange.
- Articles on the company.
- Insider trading. Pay more attention to the insider purchases at market prices. Use common sense.
- Groups helps you to determine whether the stock is in a sector trending up.
- The last line lets you to open Yahoo!Finance and other sites.

Links
Expected P/E:
http://www.tonyp4idea.blogspot.com/2012/06/mysteries-of-pe.html
PEG: http://en.wikipedia.org/wiki/PEG_ratio

Short %:
http://www.investopedia.com/university/shortselling/shortselling1.asp#axzz2LNDvpemo

Blue Chip Growth:
http://navelliergrowth.investorplace.com/bluechip/password/index.php?plocation=%2Fbluechip%2F

Openinsider: http://www.openinsider.com/
Finviz: http://Finviz.com/
terms: http://www.Finviz.com/help/screener.ashx
Insider Cow: http://www.insidercow.com/
Current Ratio: http://en.wikipedia.org/wiki/Current_ratio
How to find quality stocks.
http://seekingalpha.com/article/2381395-how-to-identify-quality-stocks-and-is-there-really-alpha-to-be-had

Mysteries of P/E

If you believe you can make good money by selecting stocks with low P/Es solely, dream on. If it is that easy, there will be no poor folks. However, buying fundamentally sound companies would reduce risk and improve the chance of its appreciation.

P/E is the most misunderstood indicator. To me, it is the most useful one among all metrics if it is properly used. Earnings are the key to stock appreciation and P/E measures its value. To illustrate on P/E, you pay a million for a hot-dog cart in NYC. Even if its earnings increase year after year, you will never recoup your investment as you have paid too much even for a good business.

Better definition

P/E should be inverted as E/P, which is termed as Earning Yield. Earning Yield is easy to be compared and understood. It takes care of negative earnings for screening stocks and ranking (comparing stocks with better P/E first). If you sort P/E in ascending order, your order is wrong with negative earnings but right with E/P.

It is usually compared to a 10-year Treasury bill yield (or 30 years) or a CD rate. If the stock has 5% earning yield and your one-year

CD is 1%, then it beats the CD by 4% in absolute number and four times better. However, the CD is virtually risk free (with deposit amount limit in most banks). Earning yield is an estimated guess and it may not materialize.

Many ways to predict E/P

- Based on the last 12 months. Project it to future E/P. It is also called the last twelve month E/P.
- Based on analysts' educated guesses. Guesses may not materialize. Based on my experience, the expected usually predicts better than the one based on the last 12 months. This is the one I use most and many investing subscriptions provide this expected P/E (same as Forward P/E) or expected E/P.

Usually I do not trust the analyst's opinions due to conflict of interest. However, the earnings estimate is my exception.

- Based on the last month or the last quarter. Latest information could be better for prediction. However, they are not good for seasonal businesses such as the retail where most sales are done during the Christmas season.
- Besides the Pow PE described later, I take the average of the earning yield EY as:

The Avg. EY = (EY from the last twelve month + Expected EY + EY from the current month of prior year) / 3

It averages out using figures from the past, the present and the future. If no one has used it, I claim shamelessly it is my original idea. ☺

Best E/P could not be the best

Very high E/P could be signs of troubles ahead such as lawsuit pending, fraud, etc. If you find companies E/P over 50%, it means two years' profits could equal to the entire cost of the company! I can tell you right away they smell fishy unless you believe there is free lunch in life.

However, from time to time, some bargains do exist due to certain conditions or Wall Street is just wrong about the company. You need to find out whether they are bargains or traps. When the E/P is low (sometimes even negative) but is improving fast, it could mean big profit for you. Fundamentalists may miss this opportunity in the early stage, which is also the most profitable time to buy. This could be a turnaround.

During a recession, a good company will have a hard time to promote a new product as the consumers are thrifty. At the same time, it usually is the best time to develop products if the company has enough cash to finance it. In this case, there is no alarm even with negative earnings. The only alarm is when the company cannot meet the debt obligations.

Some companies can manipulate earnings via dirty tricks in accounting. It could make this year look really good, but it is harder but not impossible to continue the same trick for many years. Check out the footnotes in the financial statement.

E/P and PEG

For value investing, E/P is usually used and the higher the better. Watch out when it is extraordinarily high.

PEG (P/E growth) measures the rate of improving P/E.

PEG = (P/E) / Earnings Growth Rate

As described, E can be based on the last 12 months, expected or the average. I prefer expected earnings.

Which of the following two stocks do you want to buy based on their historical earning yields and earnings growth?

1. A stock has a 10% earning yield with no earnings growth.
2. A stock has an 8% earning yield with 50% earnings growth.

If the earnings growth continues, in next year the second stock should pay 12%, substantially better than the first stock. This is another reason we should use expected earnings than historical earnings.

PEG may give a low value for companies that pay high dividends. To correct it,

PEG = (P/E)/(Earning Growth Rate + Dividend Yield)

When the general market favors growth stocks, weigh more on growth metrics including PEG. I claim no credit on the adjusted PEG.

Fundamental metrics

E/P is one of the metrics you should use but not exclusively. If the earning yield is high but the % of debt is high too, then a good bargain may not be as good as it appears to be. Pow P/E considers this effect.

Some other metrics may not be easily found in the financial statements such as the intangibles, insider buying, pension obligation, trade secrets, losing market share, brand name, customers' loyalty, etc. It is interesting that most metrics change its ability to predict from time to time as illustrated in my book Scoring Stocks.

P/E variations

There are other P/E variations like Shiller P/E (same as CAPE and PE10). Shiller P/E can also be used to track the current market valuation. It is controversial and its value is easily misinterpreted. Hence, use it as a reference only unless you understand all its issues. I prefer to use two year average of the P/E instead of 10 as I believe the market changes too much for a ten year span. Currently Shill P/E does not work that well as before. It is due to the excessive printing of money.

Personally I prefer to compare a company's current P/E to its average P/E in the last 5 years. Also compare it to the average value of the companies in the same industry. The average P/E for high-tech companies is different from supermarkets for example.

P/E is more reliable for a group of stocks (SPY for example) instead of individual stocks which have too many other metrics and intangibles to deal with.

When you compare the total return of an ETF to a corresponding index, you need to add the respective dividends to the index to ensure a fair comparison of total returns. Currently, S&P500 is paying about 2% dividend.

EV/EBITDA is another way to measure the value of a company. This metric has its advantages and disadvantages over P/E. Click the above links for more information which is beyond the scope of this article.

Garbage in, garbage out
I do not trust in most financial statements of emerging countries especially the smaller companies. Watch out for fraudulent data. Most metrics can be manipulated. Recently I have a US stock that lost 18% in one day due to the SEC's investigation of its financial data.

The announced earnings may not be reflected in the financial statements you use from the web. Ensure your data is up-to-date by checking the date of the financial statements. Seeking Alpha has transcripts for the earnings announcements that would save you a trip to attend the companies' quarterly meetings.

Sector and entire market

You can find the value of a sector using the P/E of an ETF for that sector. It is similar for the market. For example, use SPY (an ETF simulating S&P 500 index). If it is lower than the average (15 to me), then most likely the market is good value and a buy signal. It is one of the many hints for market timing.

Where to use P/E
Each highlight of the following corresponds to one of my books. Click it for the description of the strategy.

My book The Art of Investing describes how to evaluate stocks and time the market. It has most ideas of most of my books. The top-down approach starts with a safe market, then sector analysis, fundamental analysis, intangible analysis and optionally technical analysis. P/E is one of the many metrics in fundamental analysis.

There are many styles of investing. In general, fundamental analysis is important when you hold the stock longer.

- P/E is important in Long-Term Swing, Dividend Investing, Retirees and Conservative Strategies.
- P/E is moderately important in Short-Term Swing and Sector Rotation.
- P/E is least important in Momentum Strategy and Day Trading.

Summary

Again, one metric should not dictate the reason to trade a stock. Compare the company P/E to its industry average and its own five-year average. In addition, many industries have cycles. If you buy it at the peak of the industry, the P/E may mislead you. Besides fundamental analysis, you need to consider intangible analysis and time the entry / exit point by using technical analysis.

Pow P/E

I modified P/E to take care of cash and debts.

Pow P/E = (P - Cash per Share + Debt per Share) / (Earning - Interest gained per share - Interest paid per share)

To illustrate, the stock price is $10 and it has $2 in cash (actually cash and securities). The real price of the stock is $8. When we ignore the cash and debt, we have to ignore the interests gained and paid.

Many companies park the cash in bank accounts that do not generate much interest today. Some cash-rich companies such as MSFT and CSCO have better P/Es after excluding the cash per share.

My official definition: The above is for simple illustration. I need to expand it here.

Pow P/E = (P - net short-term asset per share + liability per share) / (Earning - Gain from short-term asset per share - interest paid per share)

You can get the short-term asset and liability from the financial statement and divide it by the number of shares. In addition, pension liability should be included in the liability. As before, I prefer the expected earnings.

In this calculation, P could be a negative and so is E. It is misleading that when both are negative to generate a positive Pow P/E. Interpret the number accordingly.

When either one is negative, most likely the fundamental is not good. There are many examples of bankruptcy when both of them are negative. Avoid companies with negative earnings and high debt unless there is a good reason such as a turnaround. The previous GM was one of the examples in this situation.

Stock buyback could reduce the outstanding shares. It would improve most metrics that use earnings per share such as P/E. However, if the company borrows money to buy stocks, it would deteriorate the debt metrics or its cash position. Pow P/E handles this situation well if the financial statement is up-to-date.

Most likely I will not get a Nobel Prize like Shiller on a new version of P/E. It is common sense to me. I have not heard others using this same concept, so as before I shamelessly claim it is mine. Ignore my ignorance if someone already uses this simple concept.

Using IBM as an example to calculate Pow P/E based on 12/31/2013 financial statements.

Pow P/E = (187.57 - 10.62 + 98.00) / 15.06 = 18.26

Take out the gain from short-term asset and the interest paid for simplicity.

The historical P/E was 10.41 on 12/31/2013 and it looked better than my 18.26. Mine is a better representation reflecting the high debt of the company. Hence, do not rush to buy IBM only solely considering the low P/E. However, even for a P/E of 18, it could still be a good buy.

Better representation does not mean better prediction. I do not have a historical database with all the information available. Vendors, if you have one, would you let me use yours to verify any improvement on predictability on this one and the Avg. P/E described before. [Update: Shortly after I published this article At

Seeking Alpha, I found it out it was similar to EV/EBITDA in function, but Pow P/E is easier to understand.

Pow EY

As mentioned, earning yield is easier to understand. Pow EY (PEY) is based on Pow P/E (PPE) with the following modifications. The purpose is to use the financial ratios that are readily available in most free sites such as finviz.com without retrieving them from financial statements.

Pow EY = Expected Earnings / (P − Cash /share − Debt /share)

Many free sites including finviz.com have "Cash/Share".

"Debt/Share" is calculated as follows:

Total Debt = Market Cap * Debt / Equity

Debt/Share = Total Debt / Outstanding Share

Ignore the stock when the top and bottom parts are both negative values.

To be more precise but requiring more work, replace cash per share with (Total Current Asset − Total Current Liability) per share. It can be found in the financial statement.

The passing grade is subjected to your interpretation. I use 4% (=3% inflation + 1% taxes). In some cases when most investments are not doing well, ignore the passing grade and select the investment with the best earning yield at reasonable risk.

As of 11/2014, you would have avoided the big plunge of IBM and F by judging the low Pow EY due to high debts.

Afterthoughts

- Sometimes P/E does not indicate the value of a company. http://seekingalpha.com/article/185341-key-tronic-keying-in-on-value P/E is a short-cut discount model.

Links

P/E:	http://en.wikipedia.org/wiki/P/E_ratio
PEG:	http://en.wikipedia.org/wiki/PEG_ratio
Shiller's P/E:	http://www.gurufocus.com/shiller-PE.php
His 2014 call	Second link
Calculator	http://www.caperatio.com/
EV/EBITDA:	http://en.wikipedia.org/wiki/EV/EBITDA
Advantages:	http://www.wallstreetoasis.com/forums/pe-vs-evebitda

Filler:
Joke

In my first job just after the Vietnam War, every one tried to date my beautiful office mate Mia except me. If we married, then her name would be Mia Pow. She would be very popular or very unpopular without showing her beautiful face. In any case, when she becomes a mother, she will be Mamma Mia.

35   Qualitative analysis

This is the last analysis to evaluate a stock fundamentally. The next technical analysis is used to find an entry point (also the exit point) for the stock.

Where quantitative analysis fails and why

I find that some stocks with high scores fail and some stocks with low scores succeed as indicated by my performance monitor. The scoring system still works statistically for the majority of my stocks.

- Reasons why stocks with low scores perform in addition to the described in the last discussion:

  o Over-sold. The institution investors (fund managers and pension managers...) dump them first, and then followed by the retail investors. The big boys will buy these stocks back when they reach a certain price range. RSI(14), a technical indicator described in the Technical Analysis article, is useful to detect these over-sold stocks. This metric is readily available in many sites including Finviz.

  o The falling price improves all fundamental metrics that have the stock price such as P/E and P/Sales.

  o The company has turned around after fixing its problems and/or the market has changed for the better.

  o The current problems have been resolved but not known to the public. It includes resolving a lawsuit, a new product or a new drug, a new big order, etc.

  o Heavy purchases by insiders. The company's outlook is not shown in its financial statements. Sometimes the insiders hide them so they can buy more of their companies' stocks themselves.

- Reasons why stocks with high scores plunge in addition to the described in the previous discussion:

- o The company's fundamentals and its prices have reached the heights. They have no way to go but down. It is particularly true when the stock's timing rating is at or close to the highest.

- o It has reached its potential value (or a target price) and it is time to take profit.

- o Sector (or stock) rotation, particularly by institution investors who drive the market.

- o The outlook of the company, its sector and/or the market is deteriorating.

- o The stock price may be manipulated. There are many reasons to pump and dump the stock. Shorting is not recommended for most investors. However, some experienced shorters make money consistently when they find valid reasons to short the stock.

- o When a new serious lawsuit is pending, a new competing product or drug, canceling a major order, etc.

- o Downgrade by analysts. They could spot some bad events such as product defects, violations of regulations or accounting errors / frauds. The downgrades are more important than the upgrades.

- o The financial statement had been manipulated. The SEC may ask for investigation.

- o Does not meet the consensus in earnings announcements. Many times investors just over-react.

Qualitative Analysis

We need to do further analysis after the quantity analysis and the analysis on intangibles. Check out the company's prospects. There are sources:

1. Seeking Alpha.

Type the symbol of the company to read as many articles on the company as you have time. Check out the date of the article and any potential hidden agenda from the author. Older articles may not have much value. If you cannot find too many good articles, check out the articles from finviz.com on specific stocks.

Recently, I read an article on AMD and it said it may have good profits in the next two years with the game consoles. The outlook of a company is not shown by any fundamental metric which is a mess. Following a well-known writer, I bought IBM without doing my due diligence (my fault). It went down more than 15% quickly. Learn from my mistake.

Be careful on 'pump-and-dump' manipulation written by authors with hidden agenda. It has happened especially on small companies before even SeekingAlpha.com has less than its share. Here is an article that tells you to sell NHTC. There is an article to tell you to buy ARTX and it most likely is 'pump-and dump'.

2. Research reports. Most likely you can find many free reports from your broker. If you do not, open an account with one that provides such reports. Some subscription services such as Value Line provides such reports.

3. Yahoo!Finance board. Most comments are garbage. However, once in a while you find some great insights. Many times you cannot find any info from other sources on tiny companies elsewhere.

4. The most recent company's financial statements. They are usually available in the company's web site.

5. 10-Ks from Edgar database (www.sec.gov/edgar). Check out new products and its potential competition, key customers, order backlog, research and development and pending lawsuits.

6. Check out the outlook of the sector and the company.

7. Check out its competitors.

8. Some companies are run by stupid people. I received a mail that my mutual fund account could be treated as an abandoned property. I have been cashing dividend checks every year and why it could be an abandoned property. I called them right away to close my account.

   The tall and handsome guy presented articulately how he would turn around JC Penny on TV. I could tell you right away that all his tricks had been tried by other companies such as Sears and most did not work. The intelligent investor does not care how handsome, articulated, how rich his family is and how many advanced degrees from prestigious colleges he possesses. If he does not make sense, do not buy his preaching and his company's stock.

   It is the same reason you read this book. If I cannot help you to make money, throw it away and it is only $10 (or $25 for a hard copy). You should look for results, not good writing.

9. Check out its business model. Some business models do not make business sense. Here are some samples.

- Giving razors makes sense, as the customers have to buy the blades eventually and keep on buying blades for life.
- Supermarket M lowers prices on common merchandises such as Coke and it works. They make money by providing inferior products that you cannot compare prices easily such as meat and seafood. It costs me more time to shop more than one supermarket.
  Eventually there will be a supermarket in my area to satisfy me both in price and quality or at least make a good tradeoff. My time is more important than the saving. They are still making good money.
- Last week it had been brutally hot. I went to a Barns & Noble's bookstore to enjoy reading the updated books and the air conditioning. When there are more free loaders like me than customers, the business model does not work.
- Market dumping works to capture the market. Microsoft used to do it with their new Office and Mail products that could not

compete with the established products at the time. Google is following the same model to dump its equivalent products to compete with Office. Now, Microsoft is taking the dose of same medicine. As of 2015, Google is not winning. Amazon.com gives writers great deal if you only sell your digital books via them. This model will work so far to capture the market today.

Technical analysis (a.k.a. charting) is briefly described here. If the stock is <u>overbought</u> (such as RSI(14) > 60), do not buy a lot as a correction could be possible. If the stock is oversold (such as RSI(14) < 25), either the market is wrong or your evaluation is wrong. Be cautious and check again. If there is a <u>breakout</u> (the price rising above the resistance line in the chart), you may want to buy it right away as there is a good chance it may not return to the current price.

Intangibles

I give a score for each stock I evaluate. Occasionally some stocks with poor scores have great returns and vice versa. In general, the scoring system works and it has been proven statistically and repeatedly from my limited data.
I stick with high-score stocks with some exceptions and once in a while I change my scoring system to adept to the current market conditions. To illustrate, the market bottom phase and early recovery phase of the market cycle favor value more than momentum/growth. Here are some of my recent experiences and strategies:

- I double or even triple my stake on stocks with high scores. In longer term, they are consistently better winners than the average with some minor exceptions. Besides the score, look at the intangibles described in this article.
- Watch out for the stocks with outrageous metrics such as P/E of 4 or less. It could be a big lawsuit pending, an expiration of some important drugs, etc. Also, be careful with scores in the top 5%. From my statistics they do worse than the average. Their problems may not show up in the current financial statements and hence the fundamental metrics do not reflect the problems. This could be the only part of the market efficiency theory that makes sense.
- The technology of a tech company cannot be ignored even though the company's P/E is high. The value of the company's

technology and patents will not be shown in the fundamental metrics except from the insiders' purchases at market prices.

For example, IDCC rose about 40% in 2 days. There was a rumor that Google was buying the company and/or Apple was bidding on it too for its mobile technology. Charts usually would flag this kind of event. They could be a little late as the charts depend on rising prices.

- There are more acquisitions during a market bottom and early recovery. The companies with good technologies are bargains and the larger companies especially in the same sector understand their values better than most of us. These potentially profitable companies will not be shown by their scores explicitly. When corporations have a lot of cash or the credit is cheap, they are looking for smaller companies to acquire or invest. The candidates are usually small, beaten up, low-priced and having valuable intangible assets such as technologies, customer base and/or market share of the industry segment. 2009-2012 was just the perfect environment and the last one was 2003. I had at least one in each of these periods.

- The opposite is Netflix, Chipotle in 1/2012 and Amazon in 1/2013. They are over-priced by any measure. However, the shorters are having a tough time. I do not recommend selling short especially for novice investors. When their P/Es are higher than 40, watch out. Some could be OK, but usually they are not. Do not follow the herd and your due diligence will verify whether they will still go up.

Use reward/risk ratio. It is based on experiences. To illustrate, if the company has the equal chance to go up 50% and go down 25%, then it is a buy and the reverse is a sell.

- The retail investor just cannot possibly know about some events until they actually happen. For example, ATSC dropped 15% due to losing its second primary customer. Fundamentals cannot predict this kind of event. Charts can but usually they are too late unless you watch the chart all day long. Some subscription services indicate these stocks in a timely fashion.

- After a quick run up, TZOO plunged due to missing some negligible earning expectation. It seems the original climbing prices already had the perfect earnings growth built-in.

I do not understand why a company loses 10% of its market cap when it missed by 1% of the expected earnings. It could be driven up and down by the institution investors. Evaluate the stock before you act. Acting opposite to the institution investors could be very profitable for the right stocks. Avoid trading before the earnings announcement dates (about 4 times a year for most stocks).

- The following are not easily found in financial statements: industry outlook, patents, good will, market share, competition, product margins, management quality, lawsuit pending, potential acquisition, pension obligations, advertising icons, etc. That is why we need to read articles on the stocks in our buy list.

- The financial data could be fraudulent or manipulated. I do not trust small companies in emerging markets. I have been burned too many times. Check the company names such as foreign names, ADR... and their headquarter addresses (from the company profile in most investing sites) to start.

  Earnings can be manipulated with many accounting tricks. A jump in earnings from last year may not be as rosy as it looks. Check the footnotes in the accounting statements. I usually skip financial statements unless they are big bets.

- Cash flow cannot be easily manipulated. It is good information whether the company will survive or not, but to me it does not prove to be a consistent predicator in my tests, but an important red flag for companies on its way to bankruptcy. There have been many examples.

- Repeated one-time, non-recurring and extraordinary charges are red flags. For a limited test for the average of "these charges / sales" for 2007 and 2008, I grouped them into 1. The average is over 25% (AVB, AWK and Y) and 2. The average is less than 5% (CAT, DIS, ADBE and AMAT). The average annualized returns are:

	1 yr. (2009 to 2010)
Group 1	14%
Group 2	38%
SPY	22%

The data is too limited for a conclusion. However, when the average of the last two years is over 25%, you need to further evaluate the stocks and find out the reasons.

- Stay away from the companies when the CEOs are over-compensated. As of 7- 2013, Activision's CEO raised his salary by more than 600%, while the stock lost its value in double digits.
- Value stocks. Need to know why they become value stocks (i.e. few investors want to own) even they are financially sound. For example, if it is a chip supplier for Apple, there are two primary reasons for its downfall: 1. Apple is declining in sales and 2. Apple is switching supplier to replace their chip. Technology companies are building better mouse traps. They could turn around in a year or so with better products.

Conclusion
Buying a stock is an educated guess that its stock price will rise. My conclusion is that fundamentals do not always work but they work most of the time:

1. When we buy a value stock, we're swimming against the tide. Hence, we need to wait longer (usually more than 6 months) for the market to realize its value. The exception is the Early Recovery phase (see the Market Cycle chapter) and it has faster and larger return from most value stocks.
2. Many metrics are intangible and some are misleading. Book value could be misleading for established company such as IBM. The image of the cowboy in a tobacco company could be a very important asset that is not included in its financial statement.

The market is not always rational.

Manipulators and bankruptcy

If we can avoid bankrupting companies and companies losing most of their stock values, our portfolio would be improved greatly. Some companies make bad bets and lost, such as Enron betting on energy futures. Here are some signs of bad situations.

- Foreign companies. I do not have too much luck in developing countries especially their small companies. They include China, Ireland and Israel to name a few.
- When the P/E is too good, find out why. If the P/E is too bad, stay away.
- P/PFC should be greater than 0 and less than 50. A healthy cash flow may not be able to service the debt if it is huge. Hence, compare it to Debt/Equity.
- Altman Z-Score. I prefer a score above 3, a sign not to be bankrupted. However, Z-Score is not designed for financial sectors.
- Beneish M-Score. I prefer a score less than -2.22, a sign not an earnings manipulator. Both Z-Score and M-Score are available from GuruFocus.com for a subscription fee.
- Z-Score metrics are: "Working Capital / Total Assets" (A), "Retained Earnings / Total Assets" (B), "Earnings Before Interest & Taxes / Total Assets" (C), "Market Cap / Total Liabilities" (D) and "Sales / Total Assets" (E).
  Z-Score = 1.2 A + 1.4 B + 3.3 C +.6 D + E
- Skip companies with bond rating less than B.
- New government regulations such as taking out the credit for solar panels.
- Extraordinary profits such as Timber Liquidator and many banks in 2007-2008.
- Accounting manipulation: Excessive buying stocks to boost Earnings per Share, excessive loans to officers, companies betting on futures such as Enron, too many one-time charges, reinstating the previous earnings...

The current financial statements could be the best source to look for them. If you read something you do not understand, be cautious.

We need to consistently monitor our stock holdings and sell them before they lose most of their values. Recommend to use mental stops (instead of stops) to avoid flash market crashes.
Use Seeking Alpha's portfolio to speed up the process. Be careful on potential authors' manipulations even it does not happen often. This is why we need to have a focused investing portfolio of about 10 stocks; the number depends on your time available for investing. To illustrate, I have about 10 stocks with heavy bets and about 200 in regular bets. I would spend more time in monitoring the 10 stocks than the rest.

Mergers

Mergers are usually good for the merging companies to eliminate duplicate corporate functions such as payroll administration and researching on similar subjects.

The company being acquired usually has huge appreciation. I have a screen to search for the potential candidates. The Early Recovery (a phase of the market cycle defined by me) has more of these candidates. Big companies know their values and see good values when these stocks have been beaten in the market.

Then I do an intangible analysis on items that are not available in the financial statements and/or cannot be quantified. They are patents, technologies, research staffs, customer base, brand name, barriers to entry, distribution channels, competition, product cycle, management, pension obligations...

In 2003 I bought stock of a software company that was acquired by IBM profiting more than double. In the 2008 cycle, I bought ALU at $1 and sold it briefly at 40% profit. I expected Cisco would acquire it but it did not. In two years it was acquired by another competitor for more than $3. I need patience. ALU had a lot of patents.

The company going to be acquired tries to make the financial statements very rosy. A Chinese company tricked Caterpillar to acquire it and Caterpillar lost huge in this deal. Even big company can be fooled. It happens every day for buying small businesses. One simple trick is asking their friends buying the services on the first few months after the business has been sold.

XII Bonus & current events

36 Order prices

Market orders

Use market orders only when it is necessary (more later) as stocks prices can easily be manipulated especially on stocks with low trading volumes.

However, in a rising market, many fast rising stocks can only be bought via market orders. Many winners never take a breather on its way up.

In my momentum portfolio on 11/2013, I placed a sell price for GERN far higher than the market price. Surprisingly I sold it for this price making an annualized return of 1,176% for holding it for 21 days. When there are few or no other sellers for the stock, the market price would be the price you set. If I cannot sell it in the next 9 days (30 days is my holding period for momentum stocks), I would set it lower. Update: One year later, GERN lost 29%.

Sensible discounts

I prefer to buy the stock at the price closest to the last trade price (to most it is the market price). I seldom lose buying these orders. Sometimes I use the day's lowest price to buy (or the highest to sell) plus a penny (or minus a penny for sell prices to sell).

My other purchase strategy is using 0.15% or 0.25% less than the current prices for stocks I really want. For some promising stocks, I buy them at almost the market price and then place another order on the same stock at 0.5% less than the last trade price (and sometimes 2% depending on the current market trend).

We all want to pay less and sell at higher prices. However, if the market price is too far away from the market price (such as 5% from the market price), these trades may never be executed. I have a long list of buy orders that are not executed and turn out to be big gainers. Learn from my bad experiences.

Use a good discount (such as 10% from the market price) if you believe the market, the sector or the stock will dip by 10%. After you bought the stock, you place a sell order 10% more than the price you paid for hoping the stock return to the original price and you pocket 10%. Wishful thinking! However, it has happened to me several times primarily due to temporary market dips.

It works when there is a correction and/or the stock is very volatile. It is usually within the 5% range to take advantage of these situations, not the 10% described. For 10% plunge, it usually is due to some serious problem of the company surfacing. One common reason is not meeting its earnings expectation and in this case it usually continues its downward trend.

Larger discounts on a falling market
During a falling market (or a mild correction), 3% less than the current prices for buy orders may be fine for some stocks (use 5% for volatile stocks). To illustrate, I placed about 10 of such orders over the last two months during a market dip. Most of the orders were filled. When the market is plunging, do not buy any stock.

Caterpillar and Cisco are some of my buys at these discounts. They are in my watch list to buy. Initially these shares often fall even lower as the trend was downward. As of 12/18/12, CAT earned me from 3% and 14% (bought in 6/12 and 7/12) and CSCO bought in 7/14/12 returned about 34%. My original objective: Buy deeply-valued stocks, wait and sell when the economy returns.

When you predict the market to dip by 5%, set your buy orders accordingly. Again, predictions are just educated guesses. From my experience, they work most of the time but not all of the time.

On the day of the earnings announcement, the fluctuation of the stock is usually high. Check any change in the earnings estimate before the announcement and act accordingly. Zacks is supposed to be a useful tool to predict earnings estimates. Do not place orders before the earnings announcement dates. When the earning turns out to be good, the stock price surges and your order will not be executed. When the earning is bad, the stock price will plunge usually and you most likely over-pay.

Option expiration dates usually cause more volatility. Retail investors do not have to concern except using wider stops. In theory, dividend days have little effect on the stock price as it will be lowered by the dividend amount.

High volume of a stock could mean opportunity

High volume usually increases the stock price volatility. If the volatility of a stock increases substantially (such as doubling its average daily volume), there could be important news on the company, recommendation changes from a major analyst or trading by the institution investors. It usually takes the institution investors a week to trade a stock with their sizable positions.

Many times it is started by the insiders who know about the breaking news of a stock before it is publicized. Some investment services / sites specialize in identifying the increasing volumes of stocks.

Because day traders do not want to leave any open positions overnight, higher volatility occurs at the end of the day. It is the same on the day (usually on Friday) when the options are expiring.

Monitor your trade prices

You cannot tell whether you are paying a fair price without keeping a record. To illustrate, you're paying 1% less than the market prices in buying stocks. You may have missed buying some winners. If the 1% you saved is smaller than the appreciation of the stocks you would have bought at market prices, then you should adjust the buy prices to 0.5% less than the market price and monitor again.

Market trend makes a difference too. When the market is trending up, buying any stock would most likely be profitable and usually the purchase orders with high discounts will not be executed.

Follow the same logic on sell orders. Need to have at least 25 stock purchases (and potential purchases) to make the conclusion meaningful. If you do not trade a lot, you do not have enough data to verify.

Good prospects

When you find gems especially those stocks that are followed by analysts, buy them even at market prices and consider doubling the bet if you are really sure you have a winner. From my super stock screens, I spotted NHTC. I placed several bets and one market order. All of them have NOT been executed except the market order. At the end of the day NHTC is up 18% and my executed order is up 14%. I did not have the best buy but made a good profit. NHTC was on its way to huge appreciation and I sold it too early. Learned not to sell a winner and protect the profit with a stop.

Lower the bet for risky stocks even they have good fundamentals.

Quality over quantity

I prefer to research a stock thoroughly than buying several stocks not thoroughly researched just for better diversification.

Double the bet on stocks that look great after the research. For risky stocks that look good, you may want to halve your normal bet to cut down the risk. If you are less risk tolerant, do not buy risky stocks at all. My results are not conclusive on risky stocks but I do have a good sleep.

A recent example
Recently I sold EA with $1 more than my order price but $2 less than the current price of the day, which was the earnings announcement day. I recommend not placing orders right before the earnings announcement day for the stock. If the earnings is good, you do not get all the profit as in this real example; my broker did get me $1 more. If the earnings is bad, you will not sell it any way. It is the same for buying stocks.

Afterthoughts
- Besides luck, the smart investor never sells at the peak but usually within 10% of the peak. No one can predict the peaks consistently.
- I made mistakes like most of you. One time my buy price was higher than the last price executed. Luckily my broker adjusted

it to the right price and I would not be that lucky next time. Several times I switched the buy price and sell price by mistake. One time it was due to my boss was coming that forced me to enter my order hastily.

- Some experts do not suggest their clients to buy stocks on the way down. With respect, I offer opposing arguments.

  - It is fine to buy them on the way down, if you have the conviction that the company or the economy will recover.
  - No one knows where the bottom is, but averaging down could be beneficial if the company or the economy can recover. Check why its stock price is falling and whether the company can fix its problems. Some major problems are only temporary or easy to fix.
  - Most of my big profits are made by buying close to the bottom prices on stocks that have good potential to recover.
  - Many value stocks are on sale when the market dips. The most favorable time is in the Early Recovery, a phase in the market cycle defined by me.
  - Most experts agree that: The best time to buy is when there is blood in the street. It is demonstrated by the year 2003 and 2009.
  - Contrarians never follow the herd, but you need to have a good reason to be contrary. I recommended Apple in 2013 when every institution investor was dumping Apple.
  - Stocks are manipulated via selling shorts. When the shares of a stock to short (like over 30% of shorts) are running out, there is a good chance for a short squeeze. Ensure the company being shorted heavily is not heading to bankruptcy.
- Make good money when you are right only 45% by: 1. Limit your losses via stops and 2. Place higher stakes on stocks with higher appreciation potential.
- Some make money on earnings announcement (found in Finviz.com). Earnings would amplify the stock price by at least 5%. Once a while, there are exceptions. In the last quarter of 2015, Disney posted great results, but the stock dropped. It could be the market even expected better results or the market is not rational. I believe the later in this case.

37 Stop loss & flash crash

You can limit your stock loss with stops. There are some incidents that you do not always want to use stop loss.

- Flash crash (May 6, 2010 also August 2015).
  It would turn your stops into market orders that could be substantially lower than your stop prices. Some brokers offer stop limits, but they do not guarantee the orders will be executed.

  The better way is "mental stop" (my term). You do not place a stop order but place a market order to sell when your stock falls below a pre-defined price. During flash crashes, you do not want to place the market orders to sell but place orders to buy from your watch list.

  I bought some stocks at more than 10% discount during the flash crash (actually I could buy them even at better discounts) and within a week most returned to the prices before the flash crash.

  Placing buy orders with huge discounts to the market prices works better for volatile stocks. However, I did buy some of these stocks due to bad news such as unfavorable earnings announcements. The strategy of always leaving some buy orders at huge discounts is not perfect. However, I should say from my experiences I won more than I lost.

  Avoid trading drug and bio companies with huge differences to the market prices. High tech is a good sector for this purpose and fluctuating 10% in this sector is more a norm than an exception. Buying an ETF at 5% discount is a better bet than buying specific stocks from my experience.

- My experience with 911.
  I sold many stocks due to stop orders during 911. The market came back in the next three days and I missed the recovery from the stocks that were sold and did not buy back in time.

- If your stocks are rising, you need adjust the stop loss prices accordingly. To illustrate in maintaining a 10% stop loss, your stop is at 90 when the current price is 100. When the stock price rises to 200, it should be adjusted to $180 (10% less than the current price). It is also called as trailing stop.

  Some brokers automatically delete the stock orders over a certain period of time (1 month, 3 months...) even on 'Terminate until Cancel' orders, and these stop loss orders should be re-entered at the end of the period. Check your broker's policy.

- Risky market.
  When the market is risky, you may want to use stop loss. To prevent another flash crash, you may want to use 'mental' market order. It is not perfect, as it requires constant watching of the market.

  There are many investing services and sites that give you the 'right' prices for stop loss. Basically it depends on how volatile are the specific stocks. The chartists will tell you under normal conditions stocks are trading between the resistance line and the support line. Use the stop loss just below the resistance line to avoid the stop order being executed due to the volatility of the stock.

  For simplicity as I have too many stocks in my portfolio, I use a percent. In the old days, it is recommended 8% or so below the prices you paid for. In today's volatile market, I recommend 12%.

- Risky stocks.
  Stop loss is the only way that can limit your loss for big drop (such as 25%).

- Low-volume stocks.
  The market order could drive the prices right down as there are few buyers in low-volume stocks. If there is only one buyer, he will buy the best price for him (or the worst price to the seller).

Unless I have good reasons, I would skip the low-volume stocks. I define low-volume: If my buy amount is higher than 1% of the average daily amount (= average daily volume * stock price).

- Beta.
  Stocks may be more volatile than the market. Beta is used to measure its volatility. The market can be measured by S&P500 index. If the beta of a stock is 1, its volatility is the same as the market. If it is 1.2, it is 20% more volatile.

  Set a lower stop loss for volatile stocks to prevent stocks from selling due to regular fluctuations.

38 Trade by headlines

When it rains in Brazil, buy coffee futures.

Recently, it rains too much in SE Asia, so buy rice futures. I do not trade futures, so I miss out the opportunity and unfortunately there is no equivalent ETF for rice. In the beginning of 2012, we should know the farming crops especially corn will not be good due to the flooding and drought in different parts of the world. Act accordingly for the profit potentials.

When a war is starting in Middle East, most likely the oil price will rise. Buy the oil ETF and sell it when the chance of the war is reduced. Many tiny drops of profit could turn into a river of profit.

Trade by headlines is profitable, but it is hard to master and is very time-consuming. Test this strategy on paper for years before you commit with real money as in most strategies. Most couch potatoes read newspaper and watch TV all day long without making a penny. They could be couch potato millionaires if they read this article, paper test/refine the strategy and act on it!

However, the media tend to exaggerate headlines in order to sell their ads. Ignore all the recommendations on stocks. Most likely they are outdated information and some may be manipulated. Do your own research as your mother teaches you that there is no free lunch.

Rules of the game

1. Do not be too emotional; ignore your past wins and losses except using them as lessons.

2. Do not bet the entire farm. Consider option, ETFs and/or small bet on stocks, which have too many other factors to be considered.

3. Trade it fast – today's headlines will not be headlines tomorrow. There are very few exceptions.

4. Where there is a winner, there is always a loser. For example, Apple was a winner with the iPhone and BlackBerry was a loser. Same for Best Buy and Circuit City.

5. Do not forget when to exit for either a small profit or a small loss.

6. Quick evaluation. The headline will be gone if you do not act fast. Skip companies with poor metrics. Prefer to buy an ETF related to the headline. To illustrate, you should research oil before and act right away when there is an opportunity.

7. Most likely someone has used the information before you get it. However, some info can be deducted before it occurs. Insider purchases is a good guide.

8. Learn my 5-minute evaluation process of a stock (a quick way but not recommended if you have time to do a thorough research):
    - From Finviz.com, enter the stock or ETF symbol. Look at how many greens in metrics than reds.
    - Check out Forward P/E (E>0 and P/E < 20), Debut / Equity (< 50%) and P/FCF (not in red color).
    - SMA20 (or SMA50 for longer holding period). If SMA20 is > 10%, it is trending up.
    - Scroll down for Insider Trade. It usually is a good buy if insiders are buying heavily with market prices.
    - Be cautious on foreign and low-volume stocks.
    - If most of the above are positive, it is likely a buy. As in life, nothing is 100% certain.

If you have a hard time to follow the above, most likely this strategy is not for you and it is better to return to your couch. No offense.

Volatile market and headlines

As of 7/2012 (2015 too), the market went sideway and was influenced by headlines. 2013 had been volatile with dips and surges influenced by daily news. The trend was up though. The Federal debt problem, EU crisis… had not been resolved. Every time we had good news, the market rose, and vice versa. In this market, buy on dips (3% down from last temporary peak) and sell on temporary surges (3% up from last temporary bottom). Some use 5% instead of 3%.

Trend and calendar timing

Usually following the trend is better than ignoring it.

- Many retail investors want to get rid of the losers for year-end tax planning. Buy them at year-end and sell them early next year. In the year end of 2012, it acted the opposite as folks were selling their winners expecting larger tax bite next year that turned out to be false.

  This could be the reason for sell-off of Apple in year-end of 2012 and it gave us good entry point. To me, Apple's fundamentals were sound though the media said otherwise. In a few months, Apple became a value stock from a growth stock according to the press.

- Investors are not rational and follow the market blindly. The strategy 'Buy low and sell high' works.

- We have so many good news and bad news in the same year. Ensure the bad news will not extend to worse news. Timing is everything. Buy on bad news and sell on good news; it does not work when the market plunges.

- The media influence the market. Analyze their arguments. If they exaggerate them, do the opposite.

- Over-reaction to earnings missed or gained. When the company missed the earnings by 5%, there is a very good chance the stock will be down in a year, and vice versa. However, when it missed by 1% and the stock lost by 10%, it could be a buying opportunity, particularly when it was a temporary condition and the company is fundamentally sound.

- Buy the stock at dip when a solvable problem surfaces. Sell after the problem has been resolved. Ceiling debt is such a solvable problem and it is caused by politics. In the beginning of 2013, I mentioned that the debt problem had not been resolved and we would have this ceiling debt problem periodically until it will be eventually resolved.

Scheduled events

Some events are scheduled such as earnings announcements, unemployment reports, etc. Most likely educated guesses of the outcomes have already been circulated in the web.

The last five events on the Federal debt handling (using fancy names such as sequester and debt ceiling) were scheduled such as the government shutdown. They drove the market down by about an average of 5% each time. Sell before the event and buy back afterward. The Congress has cancelled these debt deadlines as of 1/2014.

Use deduction

In 2014, China has a great harvest on wheat, corn and rice. China's population is #1 in the world and its middle class is growing. The farmers in the US will be hurt as they cannot export these products to their number one customer. Use the same logic to deduct that there will be problems in the companies that supply products and services to the farmers. They are combines, fertilizer companies and seed companies. It further translates into Deere, Potash, Monsanto and AGCO.

My experiences

- When the interest rate is expected to rise, plan on investments that are favorable to it and vice versa.

- On the same week, CROX lost almost 40% in one day. I bought some and made about 10% profit in a week. CROX's fundamentals were no good and it did have a history of roller coaster ride in its stock price. After a year, I found out that I sold it too early as the stock price doubled. Better to buy a stock on its way up than down unless we identify that the bottom has been reached.

- I missed applying the same trick to the rise of Apple when Apple announced its new iPod. I should at least buy the stocks of its part suppliers. Hope learn this lesson and take advantage of future similar circumstances.

  I missed the opportunity to buy uranium stocks. It should be bought after Japan's disaster. When Japan approved the reopening of nuclear reactors today, these stocks including CCJ, DNN, LEU, URRE, UEC, URZ, URG and UUUU surge. When China's new nuclear reactors are on-line, they will surge again.

- Experiences in early 2014.
  Recently and in a short time, I made a good profit on BBY and a tiny profit on TGT. Both were bought due to headlines.

  Bad headlines usually cause the stocks to move faster than good headlines. The recent examples are LL selling 'illegal' goods and an unfavorable article from China on NUS.

39   2015, A sideway market

Market can move up or down. Usually it dances side way when switching from one trend to the other. When it moves down, it moves at a faster speed. When the volume is unusually low, it could be a hint that the market is changing direction.

Market movements could be predicted by moving averages (30-days moving average is one for dips and 52 weeks for plunges for example). When it moves above the average line, most likely it will move up and vice versa.

For volatile markets, the last time it peaks and the last time it bottoms are termed as resistance line and support line respectively. In theory and theory only, a side-way market never breaks out from these two lines. It is a prediction and many other factors should be considered. Even with all the right educated guesses, the market is not always rational.

Take advantage of the side-way movements by buying at small dips (the support line) and selling at small peaks (the resistance line).

You can take advantage of market timing by not holding a stock forever and by buying and selling the same stock or an ETF (and contra ETF). I believe the 'buy-and-hold' is dead since 2000 for skillful traders and swingers. I cannot find too many articles praising this strategy with data after 2000. However, it beats the usual wrong market timing strategy by most retail investors.

Market plunges are usually fast and steep.

2015 Update. The last time we had a down year in a year before election year was 1939, the start of WW2. Even 2007 was an up year. I had posted this info for 2015 even during the fierce correction in August, 2015. Adding the 1.9% dividend, the market beats the one-year CD by a good margin in 2015. To profit in this market, buy at temporary dips and sell at temporary surges.

40　Brief market outlook for 2015-2016

For the last few years, most market predictors have their crystal balls broken. It is due to the excessive supply of money that leads to a non-correlation of the economy and the stock market. It cannot last forever. It will correlate again when the money supply is reduced.

The incredible recovery of the market from 2007-8 is due to the excessive printing of money (i.e. money supply). It leads to easy credit to buy stock (margin debt) and buyouts/corporate profits. With more money to buy stocks and fewer stocks to buy (buyouts), it is a simple case of Supply and Demand.

2015 will be a tough year to predict. I will predict a gain of 5% if the market does not plunge. As usual, there are two camps in opposite directions.

Good News

- It is rare that the market is down on a pre-election year. 2007 is a winner with the SPY flat plus dividends.
- The market is slightly over-priced. SPY's P/E is about 18 vs. the normal 15.
- The economy is improving slowly.
- Energy cost is reducing (bad for the energy sector).
- Most corporations have good profits especially in the first and second quarter.

Bad News

- Margin debt is in the record high. The market would usually plunge the next year after that year.
- Interest rate will climb after the mid year of 2015. It will be very small.
- A market bubble is forming. It is due to many buy-backs (via cheap credit). When you have more funds (again via cheap credit) to chase the reduced number of stocks, a bubble is being formed.

- The national debts (partly due to our endless wars) and obligations (partly due to our aging population) are high as a percentage of the GDP. If we legalize the 4 million illegals, how many will give up their jobs and collect welfare?
- Very seldom we have three terms of the same political party in charge. Most likely we will have a Republican president in 2016 from this logic; do not quote me on this one. By statistics, the pro-business Republican is not good for the stock market. Ironic!

What should we do

I would watch how the above will materialize. The weather man can predict the weather in the next few days better than the next month.

When the market is down, we need to know whether it is a correction or the start of a market plunge. For a correction, you want to buy stocks as in Oct. 15, 2014. For market plunges you want to sell. For me, I prefer to ignore corrections as it could be the start of a market plunge. Most predictions from analysts and fund managers are rosier than they actually are. Accept their ideas that make sense.

Summary

2015 could be fine and 2016 could be very risky. We're living dangerously on borrowed time. Prepare yourself as illustrated in Chapter 2 and practice on how to detect market plunges in Chapter 3.

The above is written 12/1/2014. We may have a flat year in 2015, but 2016 is very risky. Will update what I'm preparing and check out the current status (the weather man can predict better this week than a month ago) in my blog.

http://ebmyth.blogspot.com/2015/03/profit-from-2015-market-crash.html

41   Politics and investing

You may ask why politics is discussed in this investing book. Politics has been proven to affect the market. For example, the market had reacted to the different stages of Quantitative Easing whose dates had been preset. The following is a more recent example.

I predicted 2015 would be a year with small profit and insisted on so even during the fierce correction in August. Why I was so sure? Very seldom the market is down in a year before an election year including 2007. The last occurrence was 1939, the year when WW2 started. Investing is a multi-discipline venture including statistics and politics. It may not always happen, but the probability is high for these years.

How to profit

2015 was a sideward market. The market reacted to good news and bad news. The strategy for sideway market is: Buy at temporary downs and sell at temporary peaks. Define 'temporary' according to your risk tolerance.

For the 'temporary market down', personally I used 5% down from the last market peak. To me the 'temporary market peak' is 10% up from the last market down. The percentages can apply to the percentage changes in the stocks in your watch list. In another words, I buy the stock when the market is 5% down from the last peak and sell it when it gains 10% or the market gains 10%. Be reminded that this strategy is opposite to market plunges, where you should exit the market totally - again depending on your risk tolerance.

The following are my purchases on 08/26/2015. I should have bought more stocks and one day earlier if I were not blinded by fears (a human nature) during this correction. Here is my proof for my purchase orders as I was asked to. The four stocks were described as value stocks in a SA article and I did a simple evaluation. As of 12/31/2015, I sold all the four stocks except Gilead Sciences. The annualized returns are more impressive such as GNW's 10% gain in one day.

Stocks	Buy Price	Buy Date	Return	Sold date
Apple (AAPL)	107.20	08/26/15	12%	10/19/15
Gilead Sciences (GILD)	105.94	08/26/15	-4%	
General Motors (GM)	27.69	08/26/15	12%	09/17/15
Genwealth Financial (GNW)	4.54	08/26/15	10%	08/27/15

There were similar examples in 2013 and 2014.

2016: Politics and the market

No one including all the Federal Reserve chairmen / chairwomen and all the Nobel-Prize winners in economics can predict market plunges. One chairman predicted a smooth market and a few months later the housing market crashed! Many predicted correctly market crashes by pure luck. One even received a Nobel Prize and became famous. However, you are glad to ignore his later market predictions.

There are at least two best sellers asking us to exit the market in 2009. If you followed them, you would miss all the big gains from 2009 to 2014. They did have a point though. However, you cannot fight the Fed. The market had been saved by the excessive printing of money and hence created a non-correlation between the market and the economy. I bet these authors (famous economists and gurus) may have not made a buck in the stock market except selling their books or teaching where his students should request refunds. It is a classic case of the blind leading the blind or diversion of theory and reality.

From their articles, they do not know the basic technical indicator. You only want react to the market when the market is plunging and not too early. That's why most fund managers cannot beat the market as most are not allowed to time the market. Buffett had mediocre returns in the last five years – I had warned my readers three years ago in my blogs/books. To me, the 'buy-and-hold' strategy is dead since 2000. The average loss from the peak for the last two market plunges is about 45%. Most charts depend on falling prices, so you will not save 45% and 25% loss is my objective.

Fundamentally speaking

The market in 2016 is risky due to the proposed interest rate hike (as of 4/15 the Fed indicated only .5% so it would not be a factor), our record-high margin, strong U.S. dollar (as of 4/15, it is weaker) and the high expenses of the wars to start. Each reason could be a good-size article. Personally I try to maintain 50% in cash and would flee the market if my technical indicator tells me so.

Politically (and statistically) speaking

The election year is the second best for the market, but it may not be this year. We **seldom** have three terms from the same political party. For that, I predict a win by the Republicans. Republicans are usually pro-business, but ironically the democratic presidency has better track record for better market performance.

The market has more than recovered since the day when Obama took office. The S&P500 performance under Republicans vs. Democrats since 1926 to 2014 is approximately:

Annualized return under Democratic presidencies: 13%
Annualized return under Republican presidencies: 6%

The market is riskier based on the above statistics. In addition, there is a good chance that we will have either a non-politician president or a lady president for the first time (more materialized in 4/16). The market usually does not favor to this kind of change. Statistics do not mean it will happen but history repeats itself more often in investing.

Critical political issue for 2016

On our way back at about 4 pm on a Saturday, the bus was full of Spanish-speaking workers. I bet most are illegal workers working in my suburb such as our malls, the hospital and many restaurants. Why illegals? I bet most legal folks would get welfare instead of working in that shift. If they work, the state would take away the freebies such as health care in Mass. The illegals do not have this option. I do not think the politicians understand this. There is no need to build a border wall but punishing the employers who hire illegals. Before we do this, we need folks to take the jobs taken by the illegals today.

What will happen if the politicians turn the illegals to be legal? There will be nobody doing these low-level jobs I predict. No one in the right mind wants these jobs when it is far easier to collect welfare. Why would politicians make this stupid decision? They want to buy Hispanic votes as evidenced in the last two elections.

In addition, most politicians side with the welfare recipients. Since 40% of the population does not pay Federal taxes, the politicians have to satisfy their needs in order to buy votes.

We should encourage folks to work, not the other way round. Representation without taxation is worse than taxation without representation.

Our high taxes, increasing minimum wage, regulations and strong US dollar dampen our competitive edge.

Some political decisions/regulations that affect the stocks

Beside the presidency and the interest rate hike(s), there are many political decisions and regulations that affect the stocks. Just name a few here:

- The never-ending wars postpone our secular bull market beyond 2020.
- Solar City (SCTY) and this sector depend on government energy credit.
- My Chinese solar panel stock evaporated when the US banned them from importing to the US.
- Any gun control measurement will affect gun stocks (initially positive).
- When Hillary talked against bio tech stocks or the coal mines, that sector sank.

- Restrictions on cigarettes if China and Russia follow our bans.
- Our immigration policy and great colleges attract the best all over the world to come to the U.S. At the same time, we need to limit economical refugees from burdening our entitlement systems.
- France imposes extra taxes to foreign investors.
- Government bailouts on 'too big to fall' companies.
- High corporate taxes boost the exodus of corporation headquarters to tax heavens for the US.
- Infrastructure projects.
- Taking out the ban to export oil would increase the profits for oil companies.
- After the annexation of Crimea, the Congress restricted using Russia's rocket engines and gave new opportunity to the US companies in this area. Besides political consideration, Chinese rockets are the most cost effective and more reliable.
- China's suppressing corruption affected Macau's casinos. Actually every major change in Chinese policy affects the world and global investors.
  Currently the policy of forcing Chinese banks to take stocks in failing companies makes me stay away from investing in all Chinese banks.

Summary

Politics affects the market. I predict a risky market in 2016.

Economy and religion also affect the market. Statistically speaking, the market is ahead of the economy by about 6 months. However, the current market is an exception due to the excessive money supply. The correlation will return to normal.

Religions cause wars as the ones in the Middle East today. These huge expenses are consumption, not investing. It will not be good for most sectors of the economy especially in the long run.

Written in 1/1/2016.

42   Global economies as of 2016

When I look at the East, Europe is burning. When I look at the West, China is burning. I'm still playing my mandolin (actually not looking at my statements from my broker). The majority of the global economies are connected. When one suffers, the rest suffer too. Let me review some economies briefly.

The U.S.

I have to postpone the secular bull market prediction to 2020 or even later. The market for 2016 is risky. The election year is the second-best year for the market statistically. I do not bet on this one as there are too many negatives. The only bright point is the Fed may postpone interest hike to reduce the risk of this market. In addition, we have produced a lot of jobs for the last four years even their median wage is far lower than the one in 2007.

I bet the market will be correlated with the economy finally next year. They have not correlation since 2009 due to the excessive printing of money. Obama did NOT save the economy as no one can by simply printing money. However, it creates more debts for the next generations to pay.

The tool has been copied all over the world and it is no longer effective. Our strong USD (less as of 5/2016), our huge war expenses, strict regulations, high national debts, generous welfare, taxes and entitlements dampen our competitive edge. The strong USD would reduce the profits of our most global companies. A heavy blow would be legalizing the illegal workers by politicians who want to buy votes.

Asia

China is suffering economically. Given enough time, China's market-driven economy will work. The current downfall drags down many resource-rich countries such as Brazil. After a taste of capitalism, no Chinese want to return to communism, which discourages folks to work hard – who will when everyone is paid the same?

Chinese are the greatest copycats. If you believe it is that simple to copy, there should be many copycats beside China or the U.S. invites the Chinese to copy. Japan, Korea and even the US (not paying Hitler for using their missile technology...) had been copy-cats at least once in moving to a developed country.

We need to protect our inventions and intellectual properties. I am not convinced they can copy our top-secrets such as the top jet fighter that easy. If they do, there is something wrong with us. Cybersecurity should be our priority for the corporations and the government. When the copycat improves their products and sells them at about ¼ our price, we are hard to compete.

Chinese has been dominated the world in almost everything for the last 20 centuries except the last three. It has saved them a lot by copying and stealing. Today, most of their big projects have a clause to transfer technology. They're willing to pay handsome fees for technologies they want such as high-speed train from Siemens. Many companies including the U.S. give out the secrets which may be paid in large part by the U.S. tax payers to China for market access. Most of China's military weapons imports are from Russia and Russia needs the cash to improve their weapons.

Japan is declining due to the ageing population and the poor relationship with China. Contrary to popular belief, India's demographics do not help. The growing population with a lot of youths is consuming all the resources that are already proportionally small.

EU

It will be hopeless for at least another year. Euro is a good concept especially for tourists. In reality, it does not work. There are too many free loaders such as Greece taking advantage of the unified currency and foreign loans. The influx of Syrian refugees is a big burden. Tens of thousands will help to reduce their labor costs but not a million of refugees. It is hard for the Catholics to co-exist with Protestants (evidenced by Ireland), so I cannot know how the Christians co-exist with the refugees with most are Muslims.

What should we do?

- Not legalize the illegals.
- Cut down entitlements.
- Reduce taxes (both corporate and personal).
- Reduce the role of the global policeman.
- Invest in cybersecurity.
- Think like a terrorist in order to fight terrorism.

The reality

Politicians will stay away from most of "What should we do" as they would hurt election. We have record-high exodus of corporations and the rich due to high taxes.

Today are we threatened by Vietnam of being a communist country? If some country does not like how we treat the minority, should they send soldiers to invade us? If their country men do not want to fight for their freedom, why we risk our young to fight for them?

With the state-of-the-art weapons, we still cannot win in the Middle East wars. Re-think our options. One option is let them resolve their conflicts.

As of 2/2016, investors should be cautious on the market. However, we may have over-reacted to the problems in China and the falling oil price. Oil is usually in the opposite direction of the economy. However, today it flows in sync with the market due to Saudis and Russia's dumping of oil via the Sovereign Wealth funds (SWF) to rescue their economies.

The U.S. unemployment is at 5% (virtually full employment from the government's yardstick) although the median salary is still not comparable to the one in 2007. In 2007, the unemployment is huge. The recession could be spared at least for now as long as the oil price and the unemployment are stable.

Page 240

43   Tom's conservative strategy

From 2009 to 2015, these conservative strategies do not work.

The following is a summary of Tom's conservative strategy as described in his profile in Seeking Alpha web site. Use it as an example and modify it to fit your investing philosophy. You need to ignore your friends telling you how much money he is making when the market is up. You also need not to tell them how much money you're not losing otherwise you do not have any friend.

Click here for Tom's strategy. Ignore the date posted as this is one of the very few strategies that are evergreen. As of 12/2015, it does not perform well during 2009 (or 2010) to 2015 due to the long, unexpected rising market. However, it beats the above two strategies by good margins in the long run.
(http://tonyp4idea.blogspot.com/2012/05/tom-armisteads-investment-strategy.html)

A winning strategy for couch potatoes

My friend John has a very similar strategy similar to Tom's. My friend is making money with the least risk. He only buys stocks after the market crashes and sell stocks when the market rises. Ignore all market pundits. It is recommended to anyone who does not have time to monitor his/her investment.

He bought stocks in 2008-2010 and sold them after 2010. It was very profitable for him in 2000-2008 using this simple strategy. However, he missed the gains from 2010 to 2015. It is unusual that we have such a long bull market. I beg he is still beating most mutual fund managers with this simple strategy that does not require much work.

Enhance a good strategy

Following the favorable stages to trade in the market cycle described in this book:

- Buy SPY in the Early Recovery phase (about 1 ½ year after the crash or use the entry point described in Market Timing in this book.
- Sell SPY in one or two years after the buy.

Here are some options if you have time to watch the market.

- Buy stocks (or an ETF that stimulates the market) in Nov. 1 and sell them in May 1. I prefer buy in Oct. 15 and Sell in April 15 to avoid the herd.
- Buy stocks in Dec. 1 and sell in Feb. 1 to take advantage of the best (statistically) period of the year.
- Buy stocks in the year before election and sell them after a year.
- Add long-term bonds when the interest rate is high (say more than 5%). Switch to short-term bonds or cash when interest is low (say less than 2%).
- If you have time, time the market by following my simple technique to exit and reenter the market.

Spend the rest of the time in the comfortable couch (i.e. enjoying life) or sip some fancy tropical drink served by some beautiful tropical lady in some nice tropical island. Not a bad strategy! Of course, the market is not always rational and there is always risk involved.

An alternative to Tom's strategy

Have a list of value stocks to buy and update the list periodically (say every 3 months).

When the market loses 5%, buy them at 2% less than the market prices or alternatively 5% less than the prices in your list.

Decide when to sell such as making 12% profit or losing 12%. If the market is not risky, you may want to keep them longer. It should work in a sideway market but not during market plunges.

John's Strategy

John maintains about 75% cash and only buys blue chip stocks at 52-week low. He ignores friends telling him making good money when the market is up.

Here are my changes for better returns at the expense of taking more risk. I would maintain 50% cash and 0% in Early Recovery, a phase in the market cycle defined by me. I would also include all stocks with market cap over 1 billion and stocks close to 5% of their bottoms. In addition, I would evaluate the stocks before I buy as some stocks may go to zero.

Jill's Strategy

Jill does not have time for investing. She subscribes to an investing service. She prepares a list of stocks to buy. For illustration only, the stocks should have Safety 1 or 2 in Value Line or VST grade higher than 1.25 in Vector Vest. When the price reaches the price she is willing to pay, she does another research with her subscription service and check the fundamental rating in Blue Chip Growth. If they are good, she buys it and usually keeps it until the market is risky.

44 Secular bull market is coming!

My definitions

A secular stock market is a prolonged period (about 12 to 22 years) that the market is heading in one particular direction. There have been secular bear markets and secular bull markets depending on the direction of the stock market.

Market cycles exist within a secular market. Market cycles last for about 5 years. The market cycle of 2000-2007 lasts for about 7 years and the current one from 2007-to now (2016) for about 8 years so far.

Within a year there are usually two mini market cycles (I call them 5% corrections or dips/surges and sometimes one 5% and one 5-15% correction). The surges provide the best time to sell stocks and the dips provide the best time to buy stocks if there is no market plunge.

The secular market cycle, market cycle and yearly corrections (also defined by me as mini market cycles) are not scientific concepts. Hence, their average durations are very rough estimates. I use 20 years for secular market cycle for the ease to memorize while 15 could be a better average.

Market Cycle vs. Economic Cycle

Understanding the Market Cycle is important to investors and the Economic Cycle (also known as the Business Cycle) is important to economists and businessmen. Do not be confused with the two. The secular economy cycle usually follows the secular market cycle as indicated in the last 60 years. With the obvious exception of the current one (2007-2016), the economy cycle usually lags the market cycle by an average of 6 months.

My prediction: The secular bull will start in 2018

Whenever a famous person predicts with any certainty that the end of the world is coming or the Dow will double next year, it is loudly broadcasted over the news. I predict that the next secular bull market will start as early as in 2018. Who would take me, a nobody, and his prediction seriously? If it does not happen, check out which ones of my many arguments are wrong and/or any unpredictable event or events have happened.

This is a bold prediction! There are reasons why it might happen and also reasons why it might not happen. I could write a book on this topic but I will spare you the details. However, let us carefully scrutinize the coming events to better clarify my prediction.

Timing is everything even though there is nothing truly considered as perfect timing. But be aware that reacting too early to a secular bull secular market can cost you money, and reacting too late to a secular bull market can miss the profit opportunity. Vice versa for a secular bear market.

Past secular markets

If the market is good, the economy would be good and every person would have a job in theory. Even the poor would benefit from the more generous government benefits and the increased individual generosity. Today, global corporations can hire any worker in any place in the world at the least cost to change the US employment picture.

I have identified the last three secular bull and bear markets (again they are rough estimates):

    Secular bear market: 1960-1980
    Secular bull market: 1980-2000
    Secular bear market: 2000-now

I did not include secular markets before 1960 as they times did not resemble today's market conditions.

In a secular bull market, every investor is a genius. Most of our stocks rise with the tide in a bull market. With the profits from the market, we spend more on disposable consumer products. During wars, most sectors fall except those making bombs, jets and tanks.

The cause of secular markets: War or lack of war

What causes the secular markets that usually last for about 20 years? My contribution to this theory is that war is the major common denominator to the secular bear markets. Though I have not read any article that distinguishes it out, I am sure the concept is so obvious that someone would have reached the same conclusion.

In the 1960s, it was the Vietnam War and the effects after this war. Today it is the two wars in the Middle East. Wars cost us a lot of resources. When these resources are devoted to the economy after the wars, the economy would grow.

After each major war, our leaders do not forget the harmful effects at least for a while. They cannot get re-elected with a new war, so there will be no major war for a long while. That's my explanation of the secular bull market from 1980-2000. After the year 2000, our leaders forgot the harmful effects of wars and history repeated itself.

Wars are the primary cause of a secular bear market and bubbles are the triggers to market plunges. Usually recessions follow market plunges. In 2000, we had the internet bubble and in 2007 we had the housing bubble. With minor exceptions, all bubbles are caused by excessive valuation and they will come back to the average value eventually.

In 2000, many internet companies had no profits or their P/Es were very high (some over 40) from the average P/E of about 15. In 2007, the market housing value was too high due to the availability of easy credit. The only exception of the bubbles is the recent price of gold which does not really appreciate that much but the dollar depreciates. The two wars partly contribute to its appreciation.

If the government concentrates its efforts on the economy rather than wars, it could detect the bubble earlier before its burst and at least the economy would have had a soft landing rather than the hard landing in 2008. Remind the politicians to avoid any future war and use your voting power to enforce it.

We should have learned from the French before we participated in Vietnam War or the Russians before we did the same in Afghan. We have been dragged many times by Israel to the Middle East wars that we have no business there.

We cannot afford to be the global policeman. Our youths should enjoy their best time of their lives in colleges or new jobs instead of being sent to the front line. The national guards should guard in case of emergency and natural disasters, not to be sent to the front line.

I expect we'll have a prolonged bull market as early as in 2018 after ending the two wars completely; still there is no sign it will end soon as of 3/2016. By 2015 and hopefully earlier, the housing problem should be resolved by absorbing the inventory and the Euro crisis should also be resolved (as of 3/2016, it is not). The politicians will not forget the harmful effects from the wars, the secular bull market will hopefully continue for the next 15 to 20 years.

War and lack of war determines the secular market to me. However, there are many other factors playing an important role. In 1974, the oil crisis made the secular bear market even worse.

Secular bull market could be postponed to 2020

The following events may prevent a secular bull market starting in 2018 and postpone it to 2020 and hopefully earlier:

1. A possible war with China due to protecting Taiwan from invasion.

    When the Chinese government cannot suppress the internal unrest and to detract attention of its own inability, it would force itself to invade Taiwan. More likely, a trade blockage by China would be more effective with the tight economic ties with each other.

2. Another probable cause for a war is the U.S. military backing of Japan and other Asian countries on the disputes of the islands near Japan or the Philippines.

It is illogical to borrow more money from China to contain China.

3. World climate change adversely affects the food supply. If the technology has not improved the production of food in the last 50 years, there would be a famine in poor countries today.

   Global warming leads to many problems such as the shortage of drinking water. India would suffer most when China, the owner of the water source in Tibet, would re-direct the water flow for its own citizens.

4. Natural disasters such as earthquakes and hurricanes. California is long over-due for a big one. Japan suffered its worst Tsunami in recent history.

5. Huge budget deficit.

   If the government continues to spend at the current rate, the prolonged unbalanced budget could never get us out of the recession. In addition, the government's excessive obligations on generous welfare, social security, Medicare and other entitlement budgetary obligations are growing too quickly and lead to imminent bankruptcy. We already have bankrupted if the US government is a company.

   The Fiscal Cliff has not really been fixed and we are still too deep into debts. We cannot pass our debt obligations to the next generation forever.

6. The trapped gas and oil could provide us with enough energy for the next 50 years. The successful extraction could accelerate the start of the secular bull market one year earlier. We're facing oil dumping by oil-producing countries as of 2015.

Conclusion

Be realistic: Re-access these developments and adjust such predictions accordingly. An accurate prediction based on current events would better assess the risk of the market.

I do not suggest staying away from the market until 2018. As before, there will be market cycles within a secular market and yearly corrections. When we are in a secular bull market, we should be more aggressive, and vice versa in a secular bear market.

Statistically, there are three recessions in a secular bear market. Is it coincident? As of January of 2014, there were two so far.

Is 2009 to 2016 a secular bull market? No, the bull market has to be correlated with the economy and the economy has not been fully recovered as of 2016. This exception is due to the excessive money supply. The money has to be paid back. Before we have our debts under control and balance our budget, our economy has not been recovered.

Afterthoughts

- I predicted a market top on April, 2012 within days.

- Signs of an economy recovery:

    1. Increase corporate profits.
    2. Increase employment.
    3. Increase housing starts.
    4. Decrease Federal deficit.
    5. Increase the growth of GDP.
    6. Rising values on some sectors such as consumers, high tech., housing, etc.

    As of 1/2014, #2 and #3 seem to be improving. #1 is OK. However #4 is not.

    When you borrow money (#4) and use them productively, you can improve #1 to #3. I have strong doubts about this economy recovery.

    We're having a non-correlation in the Economy and the market.

The following information is supplied by my friend Norman.

- Traditional theory would say 20 years secular cycle with 10 years between major pullbacks. The first major pullback was called Capital Crisis (1997-2003). The second major pullback was called Real Estate Crisis (2007-2009). According to this theory, the next major pullback will be 2017 (Capital Crisis).

- In between major crisis are business cycle pullbacks (Kitchen Cycle) approximately 5 years each. These are also called inventory cycles.

  It should be noted that these have always existed, even before Capitalism in 1720. During the secular bull market, they are muted by the positive market trend. However, they still exist.

- Norman believes we have started the secular bull market in Jan. 1, 2013. The secular 20 year cycle is based on the generations. The X generation has just moved into old age and the millennials are becoming mid-life consumers--This is a huge generation, similar to the Baby Boomers and demand for everything is going up.

- Nikolai Kondratiev would say the generational economic cycle has 4 seasons. He said it lasted 50-60 years.
  http://en.wikipedia.org/wiki/Nikolai_Kondratiev

Filler:

   # Joke: Call me irresponsible #

I told my date that I would not be responsible after the second drink due to the lack of an enzyme.

45   Simplest way to evaluate stocks

This article is NOT for beginners but for couch potatoes who have more investing knowledge. I recommend beginners to buy ETFs only such as SPY.

Many stocks have already been researched. Most are available free of charge. I start with free sites including Blue Chip Growth and follow with my simple scoring system. If you are a customer of Fidelity, try out their Analyst Opinions.

Several sources

The popular ones are Morningstar, Value Line, The Street and Zacks. If they are not available free, check out whether they are available from your library.

Blue Chip Growth

Click here for Blue Chip Growth which is free currently for stock analysis. To illustrate, enter IBM as the stock symbol. As of 2/2013, it gives C for the Total Grade, D for Quantity Grade and B for Fundamental Grade. The Total Grade is a composite grade of other grades. If the Total Grade and the Fundamental Grade are 'A' or 'B', the stock most likely is fundamentally sound. It is similar in using Value Line.

http://navelliergrowth.investorplace.com/bluechip

A simple scoring system

Bring up Finviz.com and then enter the stock symbol.

No.	Metric	Good	Bad	Score
1	Forward P/E[1]	Between 2.5 and 12.5, Score = 2	> 50 or < 0, Score = -1	
2	P/ FCF[1]	< 12, Score = 1	>30 or < 0, Score = -1	
3	P/S[1]	< 0.8, Score = 1	< 0, Score = -1	
4	P/ B[1]	< 1, Score = 1	< 0, Score = -1	

	Compare quarter to quarter of last year			
5	Sales Q/Q	> 15%, Score = 1	< 0, Score = -1	
6	EPS Q/Q	> 20% , Score = 1	< 0, Score = -1	
			Grand Score	
	Stock Symbol Date[2]	Current Price	SPY	

Footnote

[1] Negative values for Sales (due to accounting adjustments), Equity and Book are possible but not likely.

[2] The last row is for your information only. SPY is used to measure whether it will beat the market by comparing the return of this stock to the return of SPY.

The Score

Score each metric and sum up all the scores giving the Grand Score. If the Grand Score is 3, the stock passes this scoring system. Even if it is a 2, it still deserves further analysis if you have time. You may want to add scores from other vendors. To illustrate using Blue Chip Growth, add 1 for score A in the Fundamental Grade and -1 for grade F.

Very basic advices for beginners

They are Market Cap (capitalization), Debt/Equity and P/E. For beginners, stick with U.S. stocks with Market Cap greater than 800 M (million), Debt/Equity less than .25 (25%) except for debt-intensive industries such as utilities and airlines and P/E between 5 to 20. These metrics are available from Finviz.com. Do not have more than 20% of your portfolio in one stock (unless it is an ETF or mutual fund) and do not have more than 30% of your portfolio in one sector. Do not buy stocks if they are not A or B in both the composite grade and the fundamental grade from Blue Chip Growth.

46   Apple

Contrarian

I have been contrarian against institution investors' rotations several times and most times I made good money. We need to have good arguments to be contrary. Otherwise, we're committing financial suicide.

Many investors commit the same error: Invest in a company because they love the company's products. We need to check out the fundamentals of the company and its prospect. I have nothing against Apple. Actually I recommended Apple before based on its great fundamentals while everyone was dumping it. Where were today's enthusiastic analysts?

Scoring Apple

When I was writing the book Scoring Stocks, first I used IBM but its low score would not be a good example. Then I switched to Apple (AAPL). It scored almost the highest. I recommended AAPL at $55.72 (split adjusted) on April 19, 2013, the date the book was published. It is another example that fundamentals work. However, when we're swimming against the tide, we need to be patient. At that time, the media and institution investors ignored fundamentals. The best argument of not buying Apple was "Apple has turned from a growth stock to a value stock". They think they cannot get fired by thinking the same as the herd. Just garbage talk from the smartest folks!

Fundamental analysis as of 02/23/2015

	Passing grade	AAPL		Industry
Score System #1	>=15	16		
Score System #2	>=2	2		
Pow EY	>=5	6%		
Expected Earning Yield	>5 & <35	7%		5%
Debt / Equity	<.5	.30		.29
Analyst Rating	>7	9		
EB/EBIT	>5	13		
F-Score	>7	6		

ROE	>=15%	37%		27%
SMA-200%	>0%	29%		
RSI(14)	<60	78		
Price		$132.06		

Explanation
- The first scoring system incorporates many vendors' grades. The second scoring system is from my book Scoring Stocks using metrics available free from many web sites.
- Pow EY – Earning Yield (E/P) takes cash and debt into consideration.
- Expected EY, Debt/Equity, ROE, SMA-200% and RSI(14) are obtained from Finviz.com.
- Analyst Rating is from Fidelity. If Fidelity is not your broker, use Recommendation from Finviz.com.
- EB/EBIT and F-Score are from GuruFocus.com.

How Apple scores

It scores fine but not spectacular. The score from my book in April, 2013 is 5 and now it is 2. Fundamentally it is not as good as before.

P/B and P/S are usually not useful for high tech companies. However, Apple's P/B at 6 is exceedingly expensive as compared to Google's 3. When most analysts like the stock, usually it will rise in the short-term. RSI(14) shows it is overbought. To conclude, its fundamental score passes but not in flying colors.

The brief Fundamental Analysis should be followed by the following:

Qualitative Analysis includes articles for Apple. First, start looking for articles in Seeking Alpha. Large companies like Apple are hard to manipulate, so most articles are not 'pump and dump'.

Technical Analysis detects the trend and overbought condition. Many investors do not buy a stock that is in its downward trend. SMA-200 is a good trend indicator. Its price should be above the SMA-200 (same as SMA-200% is positive).

Qualitative Analysis includes articles for Apple. First, start looking for articles in Seeking Alpha. Large companies like Apple are hard to manipulate, so most articles are not 'pump and dump'.

Technical Analysis detects the trend and overbought condition. Many investors do not buy a stock that is in its downward trend. SMA-200 is a good trend indicator. Its price should be above the SMA-200 (same as SMA-200% is positive).

Intangible Analysis

Apple has lost a visionary leader Steve Jobs. I hope he was not replaced by similar managers at Microsoft, who are responsible for Microsoft's lost decade with few innovative products. Apple has a lot of cash to finance new projects. High tech business is tough as they need to build a better mouse trap continuously. When the mouse trap becomes a commodity, it will not have a good profit margin. That's one reason that Buffett does not invest in Apple. If he read my book, he would buy Apple instead of IBM. If he read my book in May, 2013, he would buy Apple instead of IBM saving his company millions minus $10 for my book.

There are bright and bad spots for Apple:

1. Apple Text Book. Imagine all students carry iPads instead of text books. Several educational apps have been created for iPads.

2. Apple TV.
   It is a loser so far with a lot of risk and potential competitors. However, the potential is great. It could give all cable companies a run for the money. Wider internet channels would make it more feasible. Will the cable companies provide these speeds to allow Apple TV and similar products to step into their turfs? Does Apple or Google have secret projects to by-pass cables' internet?

3. While the iPad and iPhone are peaking in the hardware, iTune, software and contents for these devices to access have no limit. We have witnessed how iPad helps the folks with autism

and iPhones for the blind. I can envision many other similar applications.

4. Apple moves to Kindle's market. iPad is too big to be used to read books during commute. You need to hold an iPad with both hands. The mini iPad, even making fewer profit margins, will be Apple's answer to Kindle and a good addition to cover the lower end of its product lines.

5. All the mobile phone technology is originated by the first generation (if not counting Motorola) that Apple has a lot of patents. Its lawyers will milk money from Samsung and prevent cheap mobile phones from coming to the USA.

6. Apple Pay.
   I saw a similar ad from a credit card company a while ago and not recently. Apple has a proven history of picking up some failed products and turning them into gold. It is a big test for Tim Cook who is no Steve Jobs. Hong Kong had a similar application many years ago. The advantage of that application is you do not have to carry changes. To me, this product could be the next innovative and most profitable for Apple. Apple Pay will not make a splash in the bottom line initially, but it is an important product.

7. Apple iWear/Apple Watch.
   There will be cheap Chinese products flooded in our market. However, the selling point is the prestige of Apple and its integration to other Apple products. For a similar reason, my $50 Casio has no respect even it is more accurate and more functional than an Omega costing many times more. It will be successful, but will not make a big dent on Apple's total revenue / profit. The major problem of Apple Watch is the short battery life. If you have to charge it one or even two times a day, it will not be too useful. Only social climbers would buy the $4,000 that does not function as a $10 watch. The other problem is how secured the data is.

8. The major worry is whether they can maintain the urge of upgrade. If the new enhancements would not give me reason to upgrade, I would not be the one waiting in long line in bitter

cold weather to upgrade my iPhone just to satisfy my dumb ego. It accounts the majority of Apple's profit.

9. Apple has a lot of cash. Dividends usually boost the stock price and the option values granted to the management. However, it is important to plow back to development and acquiring technologies. They may have paid too much for Beats.

2016 and beyond

Xiaomi, a Chinese phone maker, will most likely come to the USA in 2016 after conquering several emerging markets including India. Its phone is almost as good as the latest model of iPhone at about half the price. It also has a low-end version priced at about $100 that would set up a standard for entry smart phones.

Xiaomi prices the latest phone model barely above the manufacturing price and makes money in the decreasing component prices. It gains more profit by stretching the model to a longer life.

Apple's lawyer will prevent its entry that Samsung found out the hard way. For starters, Xiaomi needs to modify the user interface to avoid some of the obvious lawsuits in the USA.

Even if Xiaomi will not enter the US market, it will steal more sales from Apple. Apple has to learn from Cisco. You do not want to make China angry. If they do, they may stop Apple from selling their phones in China. Hence, you may win the battle, but lose the war. Xiaomi could be one of the companies that would force the mobile phone to become a commodity product.

When the phone becomes a commodity, both companies have to make money in the content. Today Apple depends on iPhone for over 50% of its sales. In 2016, Apple stock may face some challenges even without Xiaomi entering the US market. Eventually the smart phones will become a commodity product and they may have to face Xiaomi or other similar companies.

Summary

The following improves the odd of success but there is no guarantee.

Risky Market?
Bring up Finviz.com. Enter SPY. If both SMA-50% and SMA-200% are both negative, do not invest especially when SMA-50% is more negative than SMA-200%.

Evaluation value stocks from others' research
Gather a list of stocks from screens and/or recommendations from magazines. Use researches that are available. Value stocks should be kept for at least 6 months and do another evaluation then. There are many other free sources such as IBD, GuruFocus, Zacks and MorningStar.

Name	Pass Grade	Link[1]
Blue Chip Growth[2]	Total = A or B	Link
	Fund = A or B	
Vector Vest[3]	VST > 1 and RV > 1	Link
Value Line[4]	Timeliness > Average	
	Proj. 3-5 yr% > 5%	
Fidelity Analyst Opinion	>5	Customer

1   Links. Just Google the Name and select the web site.

2   Currently free.

3   Free for limited number of stocks and free trial.

4   Should be available from your local library.

Evaluate stocks
Bring up Finviz.com and enter the stock symbol.

Metric	Passing Grade
Forward P/E	Between 5 and 15
P/FCF	< 15 and ratio is positive
Sales Q/Q	>10
EPS Q/Q	>15

Intangible Analysis
Bring up Seeking Alpha and enter the stock symbol. To prevent manipulation, only use it for stocks with larger cap (> 200 M) and higher daily average volume (> 10,000 shares).

Epilogue

I've received a lot of good responses and thanks. The 2nd Edition incorporates a lot of your feedbacks and my recent updates. Some complaints are not valid though.

- The primary objective of this book is helping you make money, not improving your English skill. Based on the techniques here, I had 50% cash (should be 100% if I followed my charts) before the correction of August, 2015.

- As described in Introduction, charts and tables can be displayed in the full size of your reader by selecting it. I also provide links to the more important charts so you can display them on the large screen of your PC.

- I have my annuity increased by 4 folds using the techniques described in the book over the years.

There are many reasons you should write a review on this book:

- As of this writing (12/2015), I do not know any reviewers on all of my books. Some reviews were obviously written by friends and family members.

- How can a 50-page book have far more and better reviews than my 250-page book on Sector Rotation?

- I bet some reviews were written by my competitors or ones with strong bias against me being an Asian. I beg you to write an honest review.

- A best seller tells us to exit the market in 2009 when my book told you until recently using simple charts for similar period. They had so many excellent reviews from celebrities. If you followed this author, you would have lost a lot of money.

- I can take bad reviews, so I can improve. This book is about the size of three books. I bet you have got your money worth. It is organized as a reference book than a novel.

Appendix 1 – All my books

The Kindle version of Complete the Art of Investing: 16 books in one, 800 pages (6*9) or about the size of 3 average books, highly recommended. My other investing books can be grouped as follows.

- The Art of Investing. Most of my books including its sequel Themes in Investing are based on. The Kindle version has over 700 pages. It covers most topics in investing.

  The alternate combination is Debunk the Myths in Investing and its sequel Investing Strategies: Profitable & Updated. These are the original versions.

- The following books are in a series: Finding Profitable Stocks, Market Timing and Scoring Stocks (or Modern Security Analysis: Simple & Effective).

- Books for today's market: Profit from 2016 Market Crash and Best Stocks (check current offers).

- Books on strategies: SuperStocks, Sector Rotation, Momentum, Dividend, Penny & Micro Stock, Swing and Retiree.

- Books for advance beginners: billionaire (perfect gift for recent college graduates and they will thank you when they become billionaires), Investing for Beginners, Profit via ETFs, Buffett, Ideas, Conservative and Top-Down.

- Miscellaneous. Lessons in Investing. Investing Strategies. Global Economies. Buy Low and Sell High. Buy High and sell Higher. Buffettology. Technical Analysis. Trading Stocks. A Nation of No Losers. Several books on travel.

- Concise Editions and Introduction Editions are available at very low prices and are competitive to books of similar sizes (50 pages) and prices ($3 range).

For paperback & Nook. Search my books with "Tony Pow".
My blog (www.TonyP4Idea.blogspot.com).

Links are subject to changes without notices.

Appendix 2 – Complete Art of Investing

Instead of buying 16 books, why not buy one book (Complete The Art of Investing) consisting of 16 books? Besides saving money and your digital shelve space, it gives you quick reference and concentration on the topic you're currently interested in. It covers most investing topics in investing excluding speculative investing such as currency trading and day trading.

The Kindle version has over 800 pages (6*9), about the size of three books of average size. With the cost of $10 (no promotion as this price is already BIG bargain) and at least 1,000 investing ideas, it is less than one cent per idea. Most books have only a few ideas in the entire book.

This book is based on "the Art of Investing" and its sequel "Investing themes". It also includes the abstracts of many other books. It consists most of my investing experiences plus more than one hundred investing books I read.

The 16 books
This book "Complete Art of Investing" is divided into 16 books as follows. Click for the link to the book described in Amazon.com. I squeezed more than 3,000 pages into 800 pages by eliminating duplicated information such as evaluating stocks.

Book No.	Amazon.com
1	Beginner & Billionaire
2	Finding Stocks
3	Evaluating Stocks
4	Scoring Stocks
5	Trading Stocks
6	Market Timing
7	Strategies
8	Sector Rotation
9	Insider Trading
10	Penny Stocks & Micro Cap
11	Momentum Investing
12	Dividend Investing
13	Technical Analysis

14	Investing Ideas
15	The Economy
16	Buffettology

The book links are subject to change without notice.

"Beginners & Couch Potatoes" is for beginners and couch potatoes, who can use the advanced features of this book in the simplest and less time-consuming techniques. Most advance users can skip this section unless they want to use some of the short cuts described.

We start with the basic books Finding Stocks, Evaluate Stocks, Trading Stocks and Market Timing. You can select and start with one of the many styles and strategies in investing such as swing trading and top-down strategy. Many tools are described in other books such as ETFs, technical analysis, covered calls and trade plan.

Many books start with "Why" to lure you to read more and are followed by "How" and then the theory behind the book.

Many books have common chapters such as Market Timing, Finding Stocks and Scoring Stocks. That's the reason I can squeeze over 2,000 pages into this book. Currently the printed version is not available due to the expensive paper cost for this lengthy book.

If the book you're reading is beneficial to you, imagine how it would with 800 pages.

#
The following are from readers of this book, "Debunk the Myths in Investing" or "The Art of Investing", which this book is derived from. As of 9/2016, I do not know the reviewers.

"Debunk the Myths in Investing is an all-encompassing look at not only the most salient factors influencing markets and investors, but also a from-the-trenches look at many of the misconceptions and mistakes too many investors make. Reading this book may save not only time and aggravation but money as well!"

By Joseph Shaefer, CEO, Stanford Wealth Management LLC. 11/2013.

"'Debunk the Myths in Investing' is an interesting book that on its 500 pages offer a lot of knowledge related to investing world and many practical advices, so I can recommend its reading if you're interested in this topic."

By Denis Vukosav, TOP 1000 REVIEWER 3/2014.

"490 pages of a genius's ranting and hypothesis with various theories throughout, written light-heartedly with ample doses of humor... Excellent market timing strategies. Yes, the myth of not being able to profitably time the market is BUSTED..." By Abe Vigoda 7/2014

"I just bought this book due to the woes of opening market 2016 and being brand new to investing, my eyes were crossed with all the different reasons we were/ are and what one can do to "manipulate the market". Investment Advices just to his research is phenomenal and doesn't overwhelm with big words or catchy "sales-like" tactics.

I truly believe this ordinary man, Mr. Tony Pow, has a gift of explaining his experience as an investor without the bull crap of trying to make you buy his stuff. He seemingly just wants to share his knowledge, tips, and clarity of definitions for the kind of folks like me who want to understand something FIRST before jumping in with emotions of trying to make a boat load of money. I like the technical analysis side he brings.

Mr. Tony Pow talks about hidden gems in his book, well....quite frankly, he is a hidden gem. Thank you and I will also post my comments about this author to my Facebook page!" – JB on this book 1/2016.
– JB on this book, Jan. 2016.

"Excellent book, recommend to all investors... great knowledge. It has fine-tuned my investing strategies... Your book is hard to set aside, as I read it all the time learning good techniques and analysis of stocks, ETF... Since I purchased your book in March, I have underlined, highlighted and placed tabs on top of pages for quick reference." – Aileron on this book, July, 2016.

Appendix 3 - Our window to the investing world

This is a summary of the web sites described in this book and the web sites you may want to refer to. Click on the sites and a brief comment may be included. The paperback version of this chapter can be found in the following link.

http://ebmyth.blogspot.com/2013/11/web-sites.html

- **General**
  Wikipedia / Investopedia /Yahoo!Finance / MarketWatch / Cnnfn / Morningstar /

  CNBC / Bloomberg / WSJ / Barron's / Motley Fool / TheStreet

  Understanding the news is fine but most likely you will not profit directly from the news. Read the chapter on Headlines to interpret the news and profit from it.

- **Evaluate stocks**
  Finviz / SeekingAlpha / MSN Money / Zacks / Daily Finance / ADR / Fidelity / BlueChipGrowth / Earnings Impact / OpenInsider / NYSE / NASDAQ / SEC /

  SEC for 10K and 10Q (quarterly) reports required to file for listed stocks in major exchanges.

- **Charts**
  BigCharts / FreeStockCharts / StockCharts /

- **Screens**
  Yahoo!Finance / Finviz / CNBC / Morningstar /

- **Besides stocks**
  123Jump / Hoover's Online / FINRA Bond Market Data / REIT / Commodity Futures /

  Option Industry

- **Vendors**
  AAII / Zacks / IBD / GuruFocus / Vector Vest /

Fidelity / Interactive Brokers / Merrill Lynch /

Fidelity has extensive research and I feel they have excellent executions in trades. Interactive Brokers is least expensive to trade options and their interest rates are low. Merrill Lynch provides 30-commission free trades per month for a deposit requirement in the bank; check their current offer.

- **Economy.**
  Econday / EcoconStats / Federal Reserve / Economist /

- **Misc.**
  Dow Jones Indices / Russell / Wilshire /

  IRS / Wikinvest /

  ETF Database / ETF Trends /

  Nolo (estate planning) / AARP /

I prefer to use a spreadsheet to maintain my portfolio instead of using Wikinvest or one of the many web sites that have this function. My broker has done a good job in tracking the profit/loss and performance. I use Yahoo!Finance to update the stock prices in my portfolio. This also helps me to monitor the performances of individual fundamental metrics and the screens I use. AARP is a good site for retirees. However, they are more interested to sell you Medicare supplement insurance.